THE
TRUSTED
LEADER

Use the Partnering Approach
to Become *the* Trusted Leader
People Want to Follow

SUE **DYER**

The Trusted Leader © 2022 Sue Dyer

 Published by Pendulum Publishing
291 McLeod Street, Livermore CA 94550

Senior Editor: Rick Wolff
Cover and book design by A. Kate Reynolds
Graphic designs by Bruce Wiggs
Book Launch Director: Amber Vilhauer

ISBN: Hardcover   978-1-955940-00-9
       eBook   978-1-955940-01-6
       Audio   978-1-955940-02-3

Library of Congress Control number 2021917628

*To all the leaders who aspire to become Trusted Leaders
and build their business, community, and world
based on high trust relationships.*

CONTENTS

INTRODUCTION

This book is not just another leadership book with theories about leading your business. There are thousands of those books on the market. Instead, this book is about how to *think* and *act* so you can create an atmosphere of trust, so people will follow you. By definition, to be a leader, you MUST have followers. And following is 100% voluntary. Your employees, customers, vendors, and peers will only follow you if they trust you. Their desire to follow you is what makes you a Trusted Leader. And you must become a Trusted Leader if you want to build a Trusted Business and create a competitive advantage that no one in your market can match.

This book is based on 35 years of experimentation with over 48,000 leaders. I have been on this Trusted Leader journey for four decades, and it has been the most rewarding time of my life. I am beyond excited to share with you what I've learned along my journey, and hope that you create the same extraordinary results that I have seen and enjoyed. In this book, you are the hero of the Trusted Leader journey. I am thrilled about the journey you are about to start.

You will notice that throughout the book I have either left out or changed the names of the people and businesses involved. This is because I often work at companies with a great deal of turmoil, and in my role as facilitator I am expected to keep what happens private. But many of these leaders rose to the occasion and did extraordinary things that deserve to be shared, and while some of the circumstances may be hard to believe, everything within these pages is true.

> A **TRUSTED LEADER** is someone who knows that his/her primary role is to develop and maintain an atmosphere of trust with the employees, customers, and vendors. It is only in this kind of atmosphere that a business or team can co-create extraordinary results.
>
> **THE PARTNERING APPROACH** is a two-step business paradigm that sets up the intentions and the mindset needed to create a high-trust business culture. The intentions help you think like a trusted leader, and the mindset values help to create the behaviors needed in a high-trust culture.

For over three decades, I worked with leaders on over $180 billion worth of construction projects, helping them to create a high-trust, high-performing atmosphere. Building a project takes dozens of different businesses coming together to form a team. This was a perfect proving ground. Let me just say, if it works for construction, it can work for your business and industry. Construction is a very large, complex, adversarial, ever-changing industry. There are small, medium, large, and mega-sized businesses. There are specialists and generalists. There are service, technical, and product businesses. The approach outlined in this book will work for you regardless of your size or industry.

To get the most out of this book, I encourage you to do three things:

1. Learn the Partnering Approach.

2. Take the Trusted Leader Profile and discover your style along the Leadership Continuum.

3. Practice the Partnering Approach daily in your business to become a Trusted Leader.

Business has changed and continues to change. How we lead must change too. Leaders that can create a high-trust business will always have a competitive advantage. Those who can't, won't.

CHAPTER 1:
It Started with a Fistfight

Life is an experiment.
RALPH WALDO EMERSON

During the first meeting I attended for the Association, there was a knock-down-drag-out fistfight. This was the moment when all my life's experiences came together, and I found my life's purpose. The Association was made up of 200 construction companies. They were fierce competitors. The owners of these companies joined together to protect their industry. They were people who had come up through the ranks and created a successful business based on their own tenacity, risk taking, and experience. I was to become their leader.

Facing Fear

My journey to becoming the Association's leader began with a personal struggle to find inner peace. When my daughter Jennifer was born, they brought her to me and she was beautiful—bald, but beautiful. But it wasn't long before reality came crashing in, and the pediatrician told me that

Jennifer did indeed have the same genetic blood disease that my son and her father have. At two weeks, she had her first blood transfusion. I held her for 15 hours straight while she had that transfusion because I didn't want her to be strapped down. She wasn't allowed to cry; if she did the blood went back up into the tube. Now that is a feat, not to have a baby cry when she is being tortured!

For the first few months of her life, she would go from being awake 17 hours in a row to sleeping 20 hours a day. Then my daughter would have another transfusion, which "juiced" her up again. And so it went for three and a half years. Some times were better than others, some were much worse. She was in and out of the hospital constantly. She had other complications, and her immune system was severely compromised. My poor son, who had a very mild case of the blood disease, and I would drive 30 minutes back and forth, almost daily, and sit in the doctor's office or hospital waiting rooms. I really think that is why he became a physician—a pediatric immunologist allergist.

When Jennifer was three, the doctor told me that there just wasn't anything more they could do for her. I began to read every book I could find on nutrition. My son and I dug up our backyard and planted an organic garden. I took Jennifer off all medications (they only treated her symptoms, because there was no medication to cure her disease). In six months, her blood level was stable. It was still low, but it was stable enough for her to get along pretty well. We began to have a normal life.

This experience allowed me to discover an inner strength that I never knew I had. I had faced my worst fear and had come through the other side. I now knew what love really meant; that you have to go on and do what you must no matter what. There is no option when you have a sick child. Sometimes I would feel that I couldn't make it through another hour, so I would set the timer for five minutes. I knew I could survive for five minutes. Then I would set it again, and again. I was forced to live in the present moment, and I learned that in the present everything is possible.

Now I had another challenge set before me. My husband and I had succumbed to the stress. I don't think we even realized it until it was too late. Our marriage ended. Suddenly I was facing another nightmare. My childhood sweetheart and I would not end up together. I had two small children. I needed a job!

One night when I was lying in bed, feeling like I couldn't go on, a strange calm and realization came to me. At that moment, I realized that my life's purpose was to take the strength I had found, along with what I had learned about love, into places where love was not common—that I was to light the path for others to follow.

Becoming a Leader

I always trust that God will provide. So, I waited for an opportunity to appear. In just a few days, it did. A friend asked me if I would be interested in working for a construction trade association. I said yes. I started to work the following week.

Bill, the executive director of the Association, was a person everyone loved and hated. He came from a well-known construction family and was proud of being the ne'er-do-well of the clan (he was still rebelling at the age of 50). When I came to work there was a staff of six. Bill would go on tirades, yelling and screaming at the staff, sometimes threatening them and throwing things. Within two months there was no one left but Bill and me.

After the last person packed a box of belongings and walked out the door, Bill called out her name. When no one responded, Bill came out to the front office where I sat. I explained that she had packed up and left. He sat down, dumbfounded. He asked me if I was going to leave. I told him that I would stay under certain conditions: that I would hire and fire the staff, that he would treat me and the staff with respect, that I would set the rules for the office, and that he would follow them. He agreed.

I was made the assistant executive director. I hired staff and began to run the daily activities of the Association. Bill still appeared as the figurehead of the group and ran the official meetings. This continued for some time. He would occasionally go on rants, but I would protect the staff. One time during a rant, he brought a gun with him into my office. I can still hear my staff running down the hall yelling "He's gonna kill her!" I knew that he wouldn't because this was a fairly regular pattern, he always backed down and cooled off. I also knew that at this time in the world of construction, if I let him bully me, then he would lose respect for me and I would become completely ineffective. So I never backed down whether to a boss, a union leader or a member. I also was *never* aggressive either. I stood my ground and tried to understand what they needed.

One day, when the Association was in financial trouble, the board of directors held a special, private meeting. While the board of directors appreciated what Bill had contributed to the Association, they decided it was time to ask Bill to retire. After some drama, he finally agreed.

The board of directors now needed a new executive director. I went to the president and told him that I was not going to rescue the Association just so they could hire a man as executive director, and that I just wanted a shot (I still had two kids at home that I had to take care of). All I wanted was six months. He agreed. At the board meeting, he recommended that I be made the executive director. Some thought I should be the executive secretary, but I held out for the title that fit the job. I also held out for a salary commensurate with the position. I became the first woman in the United States to be the head of a major collective bargaining group in construction.

Using the Partnering Approach

Within three months we were in the black. And I began to think about our mission, and the culture that we wanted to develop for the Association and the industry. I knew that the dog-eat-dog, fistfighting, competitive world was not the only way to do business. I believed that, in fact, by trusting and cooperating you could be just as successful, maybe even more so. I believed that if we could instill this trust mindset into the Association that we would be more successful than if we fought for everything we wanted. I developed the Partnering Approach, where we led by developing trust. Over the next few years, we took the Partnering Approach to solving the problems facing the group. We were enormously successful.

Our first Association committee is a prime example of how we solved problems using the Partnering Approach.

"Committees have never worked, and this one won't work either," Sam said.

I responded, "Just give it a try. What is the worst, most unfair requirement that you face in the industry?"

The ten committee members talked about it for a time and then all agreed that it was a specific requirement of a local water district. Juan said, "Contractors have been suing the water district for over 20 years on this requirement, and they have all lost." Juan himself had just finished suing the water district on this very issue and lost. Juan and the others just didn't believe that it was possible for this requirement to ever be changed.

I asked, "But, if it were to be changed, what would you want to replace it with? It must be fair to everyone involved." The committee worked over the next two months to create a requirement that they felt was fair. Afterwards, I invited the water district to lunch, including our proposed new language and why we thought their current requirement was unfair with the letter of invitation.

Three weeks later, 20 people attended our lunch at a nearby hotel. I explained to the water district's team that we felt that there was an unfair requirement in their contracts, and that we had some suggested language we would like to have replace the old unfair requirement. The spokesman for the water district said, "We agree that this requirement is unfair, we've thought so for years, but no one has ever asked us to replace it before. We agree to replace it with your new language."

In an instant, what was believed to be impossible *happened*. No one believed that the water district would ever change their spec. They had no reason to. They won every claim, even when it went to court. They appeared to be right. The reason that it worked in this instance was because, we took a completely different approach. There was no project involved. We proposed something that was fair to everyone. We asked the water district to do the right thing for the industry. And they did.

This was just the beginning of the committee's ability to do the impossible. This is the power of the Partnering Approach's principles and values. You will recall that the Partnering Approach is a two-step business paradigm that sets up the intentions and the mindset needed to create a high-trust business culture. The intentions help you think like a trusted leader, and the mindset values help to create the behaviors needed in a high-trust culture.

The Partnering Approach was the beginning a new kind of Trusted Leadership that, for the people who learned how to use it, really transformed the industry and what was possible to achieve. The Association used the Partnering Approach in negotiating our collective bargaining agreements, in working with cities, counties, and the state, and in all of our committees. They regularly achieved what others thought was impossible.

During one negotiation meeting, the executive director from another trade association asked me, "How do you always get your way?" Of course, it was not my way. I was by using the Partnering Approach and doing what was right, fair, and good for all concerned, while refusing to be an adversary. This is how I was able to lead diverse groups of people toward an agreed upon outcome. I've also used this approach for thousands of issues, disputes, projects, initiatives, and businesses over the years. It is amazing when people see that they *can* achieve what they thought was impossible.

Having a Living Laboratory

When I left the Association to start my own business, I set out to prove that the Partnering Approach could create Trusted Leaders in other situations as successfully as it did in the Association. I ran ten different nonprofits. I consulted for years with large and small businesses. Mostly, I used construction as my living laboratory. It is large, complex, and highly adversarial. It also is project based, so I experimented to see what worked and what didn't work and continued to hone my model until I had an approach that was highly probable to produce results. I know that if the Partnering Approach works in construction, it can work for you; it truly can work anywhere!

Over the past 35 years, I have seen this Partnering Approach allow leaders to create solutions to problems that everyone believed were impossible to solve, and achieve success at a rate that simply wouldn't be possible with a different approach. The Partnering Approach has created Trusted Leaders in large and small businesses, cities, counties, state agencies, corporations, partnerships, and sole proprietors, and it has worked for airports, hospitals, schools, neighborhoods, and nonprofits. I have seen Trusted Leaders heal rifts between people that had gone on for generations. I continually see people who become Trusted Leaders become the superstars in their businesses/organizations and begin to rise because they create extraordinary results, far beyond what was thought possible. This is my wish for you.

CHAPTER 2:
How Fear Makes It Impossible to Lead

*He who does not trust enough
will NOT be trusted.*

LAO TZU

Fear Shows Up as Poor Communication

Over a ten-year period, I conducted a personal anecdotal study. I asked over one thousand team leaders, "From your experience, what makes one project succeed, and another fail?" Over 95% of the respondents said that good communication was the reason for their success, and poor communication was the reason for their failure. After working with these teams, and learning more, I gained some real insights from this study: fear routinely shows up as poor communication, and trust appears as good communication. I realized that communication was just a *symptom* of the level of trust they had on their project team, and *communication* is what people "see," because trust and fear play out in our behaviors.

When you think about your business, remember: the number one way that fear shows up is as poor communication. And things tend to play out from there. When people don't speak openly, the rest of the team is left in the dark to try and figure things out. People are often too shy to ask questions, especially if they are confused or fearful. This is stressful, because inevitably they are afraid that they will guess wrong—and of course they will, because they are making assumptions in a vacuum. Fear makes it impossible to lead. You simply can't lead if people aren't willing to talk and share their perspective or concerns. In this atmosphere, our "monkey mind" makes up stories about why others aren't sharing. This in turn creates more fear, and the vicious cycle continues to snowball.

The Leadership Continuum

One dreary Saturday morning 15 years ago, I sat at my desk at home, looking out at the rain falling. I was preparing partnering sessions for three different teams. All the teams were overwhelmed by conflict and commotion. The people were smart, seasoned, and capable, but they just could not get out of their own way. While I sat there looking at the rain, I asked myself, "If I had a magic wand that I could use to change everything for these teams, what would I change?" The answer came immediately: "I would change how we lead our teams and businesses."

The teams' leaders seemed to add fuel to the fire, and even expected their people to put up a fight to gain as much as they could against the "other side." Some wanted to "win." Some wanted to "protect." Some wanted to "make them pay." Some wanted to compete and "prove they were better." This prevailing adversarial mindset was rampant and undermined even the best and brightest teams.

I had worked with over a thousand different teams by this point, and I saw this pattern every day. I also saw it in the expectations of the leaders, and the way leaders were trained and mentored. They were told their role was to drive the team to achieve the goals or key performance indicators. To make the sales and profit numbers. To make sure that their team was on time and on budget, and that the quality was high. Not to mess up!

I thought to myself that morning: If we could change the paradigm from being adversarial and fear based, to one of TRUST, oh my, that would change everything. The Trusted Leader Continuum was born that day.

FIGURE 1: Leadership Continuum

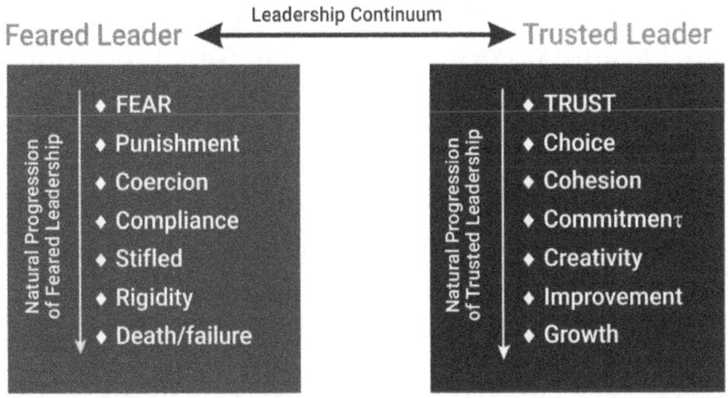

Feared Leader	Leadership Continuum	Trusted Leader
Natural Progression of Feared Leadership	◆ FEAR ◆ Punishment ◆ Coercion ◆ Compliance ◆ Stifled ◆ Rigidity ◆ Death/failure	Natural Progression of Trusted Leadership	◆ TRUST ◆ Choice ◆ Cohesion ◆ Commitment ◆ Creativity ◆ Improvement ◆ Growth

Most people, when they think of a leader, think of someone who has authentic power. They are the person in charge. They are the decision maker. And therefore, they are the leader. But my definition of a Trusted Leader is a little bit different. In order to be a leader, you must have followers, and following is 100% voluntary. People only follow you when they trust you.

What I've seen over the years is that there is a continuum of leadership. On one end, you have the Feared Leader, and on the other end, you have the Trusted Leader.

The Feared Leader

Let me walk you through the left side of the Leadership Continuum (Figure 1): the Feared Leader. Imagine, I get a job and I'm working with a Feared Leader. I'm just starting this job, and I have a 13-year-old with braces on his teeth. I've got a mortgage. I'm happy to have the job. Especially now, when so many people are out of work. I'm not there very long, maybe five minutes, before I realize: Hmm, in this company (or division, department, etc.), I better do what I'm told, because if I don't do what I'm told, I'll be punished. I start to feel afraid. Fear is the overarching culture when you work for a Feared Leader. The operating system is built around fear. I don't want to be punished. I am new at my job. I want to be here; I don't want to lose my job. And you see everyone else operating in that same manner, so you do what you're told. You may be a very skilled, and may have been very, very successful someplace else doing something very similar. You may even feel like your experience brings an element of advantage to the table, but you do what you're told, because that's what the company culture tells you that you need to do. You're following through, but you feel like you're really being forced to do something in a way you don't think is the best way to do it.

So, you feel a bit coerced. Coercion seems to be the way the business operates. You step in and follow the business norms. Your way of leading the people who report to you is to coerce them to do what you want them to do; that is how the operating system works. Over time, everybody just learns what they're supposed to do, and they go along with it. "Okay, you jump here, you jump there." When you look around and everyone is complying with whatever they're told to do, it seems like everything is going well. It's a well-oiled machine.

When I see this behavior in an organization, I ask, "How is your communication?" Remember, this is how fear often shows up. "How are your meetings? Do you ever talk? How do you know what other people are doing? Do you know what other divisions are doing? Do you know what's going on?"

They all say, "No, we don't need meetings. They are a waste of time; there isn't anything to talk about. We just focus on our own job; we don't need to talk to those people."

Communication becomes very stifled and shunned because people aren't going to share the problems they see or any ideas they have for improving—that is much too risky. There's probably punishment for doing so.

Everything works okay until a problem arises, and of course problems always happen. You just don't know when, what it'll be, or to what magnitude. So, a problem pops up. This team, filled with smart people, has hired the best and the brightest. They see the problem; they understand the problem. If you asked them, they could probably come up with 20 different ways to solve the problem. But unfortunately, not one person steps up to solve the problem.

It's sort of like standing in the middle of a freeway and seeing a semi-truck coming at you. You can pretty much figure out that if you don't move, you're going to get run over. And every time, from what I've seen, the team or the business gets run over. Every time. Of course, that leads to the failure of whatever they're working on, the failure of the team, and it can wipe out the whole business, the whole organization. I've seen this play out over and over.

In the construction industry, when they have failures like this, they do very detailed forensic studies. I analyzed several different forensic studies for different failed projects. These forensic studies are some 3,000 pages of detailed data and findings. What I found is that every single time there was a project that ended up needing a forensic study—in other words, a failed project—there was always a Feared Leader at the top and the "fear effect" took hold. Everyone involved in these projects recognized the problem, they even had ideas for solving it, *but nobody communicated.* Nobody shared their ideas up the ladder. Nobody created a forum for resolution. They were frozen; they were stuck; they could not move. On each occasion, that is what led to the death of the project, business, or organization.

I have seen the effect that a Feared Leader can have on their business. I recall one business where two executive leaders argued about who would put a note on a superior's desk. They were both too afraid to go into this person's office. So a more junior person was *voluntold* to do it. You know, when your boss volunteers you to do something. Yes, Trusted Leadership is needed at all levels.

Another time, a Feared Leader was telling me about his business. He told me all the things he wanted to do and how he was charging ahead. But when he looked back, no one was following! Ask yourself: Is your team following you?

Even good people, and their teams, can get stuck in this kind of fear culture. One of my clients believed himself to be a very skilled and Trusted Leader. He *was* pleasant—until he blew up. He wanted to "coach" his people—until they made a decision that wasn't what he wanted. Soon, everyone just waited for him to tell them what to do. Then, he got more and more angry at how his people weren't doing their jobs. He never realized that he set this fear culture into motion, and only he could change it—because fear and trust can not coexist!

Fear and Trust Cannot Coexist

Do you want to be beloved, or be "be-hated"? You may be thinking, "I don't want to be beloved; I *like* being feared. That's how I ensure I am respected, and people do what I say." Well, this is exactly what happens with the Feared Leader side of the Leadership Continuum. Let's see how it works out.

When you dictate to people what to do, they will resist, or at best just comply. But they certainly will not follow you as their leader. Fear actually creates rebellion within your team. The team you *need* in order to succeed. I see three different levels of rebellion as a reaction to a leader that develops a culture of fear.

The first level of rebellion is *hesitation*. When people fear the leader, they will hesitate at each step. They will comply, but they will not be fully on board.

The second level of rebellion is *resistance*. When people feel the need to resist, they are pulling back and just going through the motions.

The third level of rebellion is *refusal*. This is when people actually work against you to undermine what you want, or they simply leave.

I see this all the time in many different industries, when leaders get stuck in their old fear leadership ways. It's interesting, because fear is one of those things that you say, "Oh, I'm not afraid, I *want* my people to be afraid." But take a closer look. *You* are creating the fear culture. Fear is always because the leader is afraid. And look at the impact on you, your business, your team, and your customers. Some leaders believe that fear is a great motivator. But what these leaders fail to recognize is that their people are not motivated, just complying. Compliance is passive and does not engage the person if there is a problem that needs a solution. Nor will this person communicate when they see a problem, or a solution. When your entire business team acts in this manner, it is only a matter of time until a big problem comes along and takes you down.

Most often, fear shows up as poor communication, poor relationships, or conflict. These problems can happen at any level and between different groups. If people aren't communicating and telling you their truth, there's fear behind that. When you don't feel like you can fully tell somebody what you want, what you need, or what your ideas are, why is that? There is fear behind it. And one thing we know for sure is that fear and trust cannot coexist. Whenever there's fear, the amount of fear you have is going to prevent you from developing a high-trust culture. We also know that high trust equals high performance. So the more fear you have, the more you can't get the kind of momentum needed to really succeed, let alone transform your results and scale your business.

One leader was the head of a design division in a very large organization (29,000 employees). He tried for seven years to get his division to measure their performance. Each effort was thwarted. Eventually, he became the head of another division. He had the idea of developing a Partnering Approach between the two divisions and having them co-create some performance measures. There was huge resistance, until they began the Partnering Approach process and saw how they were operating in a vacuum. They couldn't improve without some kind of regular feedback mechanism.

Together these two divisions co-created 21 different performance measures that would allow them to improve the quality of their work and lessen the negative impact their poor quality had on others. Fear of change, criticism, or embarrassment had undermined this division for years. And, they really undermined themselves, because they truly believed in quality. It took a Trusted Leader using the Partnering Approach for them to be able to see all of this and take the steps that created lasting improvement.

A recent article on truth telling, published by a professor and medical school fellow in *psych.co*, said that the concept of "radical honesty" or "radical candor" is a decision people make based on their moral code. And of course, that is part of it. In the workplace, the decision to tell the truth is more often based on people's assessment of the consequences. When someone is afraid to tell the truth, they are not likely to tell the truth. Fear drives out trust. Trust drives out fear. They are mutually exclusive. Without an atmosphere of trust, you won't know what is going on. You'll be flying blind.

Entropy Is Wasted Energy

I think of this condition in terms of entropy. Entropy is energy that gets wasted because it doesn't end up moving you toward what you are trying to achieve. For example, you might have your team working day and night developing a solution to a problem only to find out that they didn't really understand the core problem, so they all created different, ineffective solutions. Or you are trying to install a new enterprise-wide application and each division refuses to use it because they have their own way of doing things. Or each division or team does its own thing so you don't really have anyone helping to achieve the overall business goals.

FIGURE 2 : First Law of Thermodynamics

You put energy into your business as resources and expect to get energy out in the form of momentum toward the achievement of your goals. The resource could be money; it could be time. It could be your people's creative juice, or prioritization (you spent time on this instead of that). Your team's efforts represent resources that are expended by your business. But what if the resources do *not* move you forward? No matter how smart or good your team is, your resources are wasted if they don't actually lead you to where you're trying to go.

FIGURE 3: Second Law of Thermodynamics

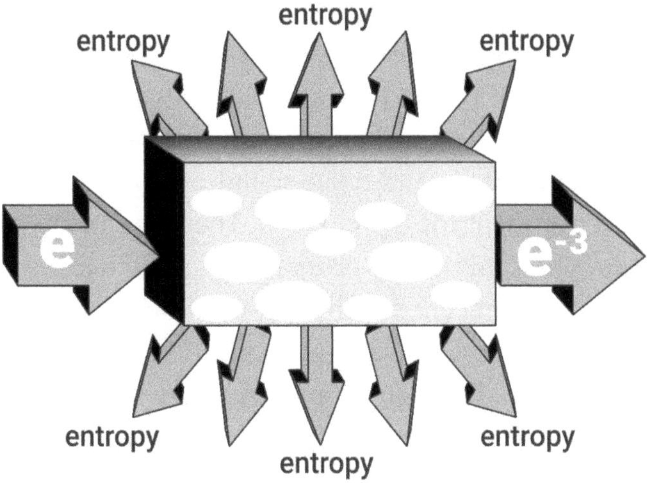

The way I think about entropy is that it is like putting fuel into a power plant (you'll see why later). The plant is a system that generates electricity. You're expecting to put fuel (energy) into the power plant and get the same amount out at the other end in the form of electricity. But what if there are leaky pipes and valves inside your plant, so some of your energy gets wasted? Now for the energy you put in, you are getting out less energy than you put in! Negative energy! Not good!

Your business is a system as well. A system that produces results. What if people are siloed inside your system, so they don't talk to each other? They don't have a desire or ability to pass information along. They protect their own turf because "that's the only thing I have control over." Or they don't share a problem they see because they know it's just going to be passed down the line to somebody else. This is entropy. This entropy is based in FEAR, and it plays out in a multitude of ways.

One day, over a hundred environmental protestors stormed one of the projects. Their goal was to stop the project from getting built by creating fear. This project was 40 years in the making. It would take all the highway traffic around a town instead of right down the middle of it. This would result in reduced air and noise pollution, and offer a much nicer environment for the citizens. There are many studies that shows that this brings economic growth to these towns. The activists threw feces at the workers and the police. They sat in the trees for weeks and pummeled the workers below. They planted bird nests to stop work. They laid down in the drains and stole the keys to the equipment. They stormed the business office. They slashed truck tires and chained themselves to trucks when the trucks stopped at a stoplight. I heard that most of the activists were not locals, and were trained at a special camp for this specific purpose: to create fear and disruption.

The team on this project did get frazzled. It was a war zone. Some ended up with post-traumatic stress disorder. Every day, they didn't know what would happen or where the next attack would come from. Nerves and tempers were on edge.

The leaders could have allowed this level of fear to define how they worked together. But instead, they made the decision to trust each other and work together to build the project, despite the fear and worry of an onslaught of daily attacks. I served as the facilitator over the course of this project. We used the Partnering Approach and met monthly to work through every outstanding issue. Some meetings were 7-8 hours long. We didn't leave the room until all issues were resolved. Yes, there were disagreements. Yes, there was emotion and frustration. But they didn't allow these emotions to define the project or how they were going to work together.

This team did many remarkable things. They brought in the city and stakeholders to make them part of the solutions. They resolved every issue as it occurred. They resolved the complicated schedule issues. They continuously addressed each issue as it came up, no matter how much effort it took. They ended up figuring out a way to cut an entire year off the project. They completed the project with no unresolved issues or claims. The facility owner wrote in an award application that the Partnering Approach saved them an estimated $50M on this project.

In short, these Trusted Leaders continuously drove out fear, and instead built a high level of trust in the most difficult of circumstances. If they can do it, you can too.

The Nozzle Effect

I found that a lot of businesses—some would say most—do not have an aligned and focused "business system," because they have fear along with the subsequent poor communication. There are many things competing for attention and priority. To reduce entropy in a business, you need to create a singular focus that everyone can align behind, and then make sure everyone is focused on its achievement. This creates a *business nozzle* where everyone is together, focused, and moving toward the same objectives.

You need everyone to be aligned behind that focus. If you put a nozzle on a garden hose, what happens as you tighten it down to a very narrow spray? Yeah, the water comes shooting out with huge velocity and force. It's the same resource, but now you've gained velocity and momentum. And that momentum will allow you to do things that were impossible before. I call this the "Nozzle Effect." This is what a business nozzle does for your company. The goal is to alleviate entropy (wasted effort and resources) and gain momentum. Fear undermines every step of the way toward achieving that goal.

FIGURE 4: Insert Nozzle Effect

For one new CEO of a large multi-billion-dollar business that I facilitated the Partnering Approach for, this was very evident when we started to create a business strategy and business nozzle. He inherited a very large expansion program that could sink the business if it wasn't done right. When I started to facilitate the Partnering Approach, I found out the leaders of the different divisions had not been in a room together in over 20 years. Each division operated as its own self-contained silo. There were turf wars over resources, priorities, and importance designations. The level of entropy was large at the same time that the challenges to deliver a successful program were huge.

The new CEO built a cohesive executive team. He had the executive team co-create their sustainable competitive advantage. Then each division created their goals with their people on how they would achieve that competitive advantage. People in the different divisions started talking and working together. They met regularly. They had a scorecard to measure how well they were following through. You could see the nozzle effect happen. It happened pretty quickly and continued to grow. They delivered the expansion program successfully. They continued to get stronger as a team and continued to build their business nozzle over the next 20-plus years, always adjusting to changing marketplace needs. I was lucky enough to work with the executive team for 25 years. They became their industry's leader. They won dozens of awards. They were continually voted one of the top places to work. They created ways to produce the highest profits in their industry and continue to do so today. They led the way with innovation. All through using the Partnering Approach in everything they did. People from all over the world came to see how they were achieving such outstanding results. They created and enjoyed the nozzle effect. You could see it in every aspect of the business, from procurement to customer service. They were ONE TEAM focused on being the best in everything they did.

CHAPTER 3:
Trusted Leaders Use
the Partnering Approach

*Trust starts with trustworthy
leadership.It must be built
into the corporate culture.*

BARBARA BROOKS KIMMEL

Trusted Businesses Must Have Trusted Leaders

How important do you think is it to your business' success that your customers trust you? Do you think people select businesses run by people they dislike or distrust? Of course not. You want to, in fact, be the Trusted Leader in your marketplace! Today, trust in business leaders (and government leaders) is at an all-time low. According to the 2021 Edelman Trust Barometer, 65% of people believe business leaders are purposely trying to mislead people by saying things they know are false. Sixty-five percent of people believe CEOs should hold themselves accountable to the public, not just to their board or stockholders. Sixty-six percent feel that CEOs should take the lead on change rather than waiting for the government.

According to the Young Entrepreneur Council, "cultivating trust and engaging in reputation management is mandatory for any business, large or small, that wants to gain a competitive advantage in our increasingly distrustful world." And, of course, your reputation is created by you, and then spreads to your team, and then to your customers. Businesses that are trusted have Trusted Leaders!

Maybe some of you are not yet convinced—you still think fear works best for you. Well, if you ever want to sell your business and have a big payday, the one thing that will increase your company's value the most is goodwill. Goodwill, in this sense, is based on how much people like and trust the business, the brand, and the management team. A business with a beloved leader will sell for many multiples over its competitor because it has created an atmosphere of trust.

FIGURE 1: Leadership Continuum

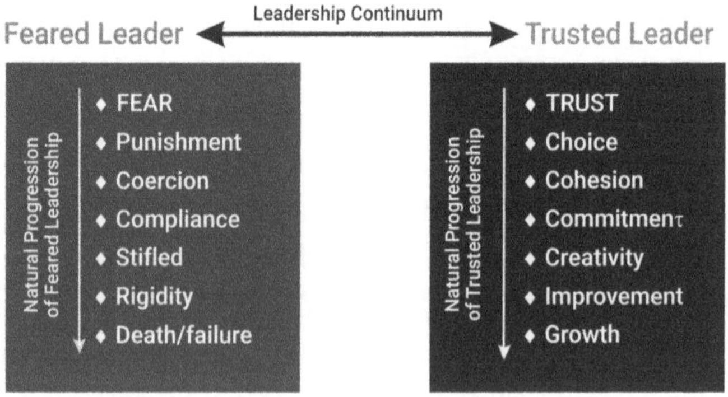

Leadership Continuum

Feared Leader ←——————————→ Trusted Leader

Natural Progression of Feared Leadership
- FEAR
- Punishment
- Coercion
- Compliance
- Stifled
- Rigidity
- Death/failure

Natural Progression of Trusted Leadership
- TRUST
- Choice
- Cohesion
- Commitment
- Creativity
- Improvement
- Growth

The Trusted Leader

It is time for us to take a look at the right side of the Leadership Continuum (Figure 1), the Trusted Leader side. Okay, imagine I have the same job, but now I'm working for a Trusted Leader. I still have the same 13-year-old who needs braces and I still have a mortgage to pay. I don't know this leader very well, but I kind of like what I'm hearing. I feel like I could trust him/her, and so I'm choosing to trust this leader. And so does everyone else in the business; they choose to trust. They choose to be a part of the business. They choose to follow.

And because they're doing it of their own free will, very quickly the team begins to feel cohesive, like "we are in this together," "we are a team," and "we're going to make things happen." That cohesion allows the team to feel truly committed to their leader, to their mission, to each other, and, most importantly, to doing whatever it takes to succeed. This allows for innovation and creativity to emerge, and leads to the overall success of the people, the team, and the business. They can accomplish things people thought were impossible!

We know that most businesses today are based on continuous innovation. The leaders talk about collaboration and innovation as being essential. But, until you've established a high level of trust, it is impossible to have innovation or collaboration. This is why so many businesses fall short. They talk about and seek out innovation, but they don't have the high trust atmosphere that allows for it to happen.

I listen to a lot of the leaders from Silicon Valley talk about collaboration and innovation as if they're interchangeable, because I think they realize that you have to have collaboration in order to get to innovation. You can't have either of them until you've created a high trust atmosphere. Yet I see many businesses create an awful lot of entropy because their level of trust just isn't really fully baked, or it only exists in pockets.

So now imagine I've got creativity and I've got innovation. I'm on my new job and I'm thinking, "This is a cool group. What could we do? What could we create? Look at this, every problem becomes an innovation." I facilitated the Partnering Approach for one team where in 30 days they installed two million dollars' worth of work a day. A normal project of that size would have taken two to five years to complete. This team completed it in just three months. They focused on creating solutions. Everybody's idea was a potential solution, and they implemented all of them because they didn't know which one would actually work in the timeframe they had or with the resources they had. They created a lot of different solutions.

Through their collaborative efforts, they actually improved the overall process. They created some solutions that had never been done before and improved the industry. They improved their businesses. They improved themselves. Improvement comes from all of this. We can come up with ideas that have never been done before, execute them in an innovative way, and create results that were previously thought impossible. I see it over and over and over again. These teams do the impossible. And of course, that leads to the growth of the individual, the growth of the company, the industry, new industries, and new possibilities.

One day, a leader called me to help him buy back his company from a publicly traded multinational company.

The multinational had purchased his business three years prior. The buy back deal went amiss when the lawyers from both sides locked horns and could not come to an agreement. The deal was close to being dead. Because of this impasse, the leader wanted to try a Partnering Approach. So I flew to meet with him and his executive team. We developed a high-trust, high-integrity approach to help both sides achieve what was important to them.

With the negotiation points and high-trust strategy in hand, the leader got on a plane and flew to Europe to begin the negotiation, working to give everyone what they needed and be fair at every step. Within a day, the deal was done. This logjam had been going on for months with little progress until the entire negotiation broke down. With the new approach, not only did the deal give the seller some strategic bonusses, the final price my client paid was $800,000 less than the amount on the lawyers' letter of intent. Both sides felt they got a great deal, and they walked away with a strong relationship. You may feel that you have little power to create a Partnering Approach, but just as my client found in this negotiation, it really only takes one person to create a trusted relationship. One side that says no matter what you do or say, I will treat you with respect, be open and honest, and work for our mutual benefit. It can take time, but eventually trust will grow as fear is driven out.

Trusted Leaders leave a legacy. If you want to leave something that is meaningful, becoming a Trusted Leader is a great way to do so. I've gone to many retirement celebrations over the years, and the one thing that stands out for me is how those leaders who were truly trusted and beloved left a remarkable legacy that lived on far beyond their tenure. I think we all want to feel the time we spent in our business has meaning beyond just making money. We all want to make a difference. I have had the privilege of working with some remarkable leaders over the past 35 years. Legends in their industry like John L. Martin, Joe Browne, Mark Breslin, Rick Land, Dennis Dunne, Mark Leja, David Thorman, Guy Mehula, and many, many more. All of them were Trusted Leaders that created remarkable high-trust businesses that outperformed everyone else. I've also seen how leaders that work to become Trusted Leaders rise quickly in the ranks within their business and industry. It is the secret sauce to success.

Local Optimization vs Global Optimization

A lack of trust also creates a crazy-making phenomenon in which teams from different divisions, disciplines, organizations, units, etc. won't work together to help the business thrive. Businesses naturally break into teams/groups as the business grows or specializes. Each team begins to create their own way of doing things. As businesses split into smaller units, people begin to feel siloed and isolated. People lose sight of the big picture. Most businesses are organized around an overall system/process for delivering the service or product to their clients. When each silo only looks to optimize their portion of the overall process, you get local optimization, not global optimization for the business—and the client.

A business must have global optimization to grow and thrive and, in some cases, survive. It will be important as you build your Trusted Leadership to continually help your people see and understand how everything they do is tied to the overall business system, and that the entire success of the business lies in their hands, no matter if they are in accounting, production, sales, or IT.

Some businesses are plagued with internal turf wars and the enormous entropy that they bring to any business. When people feel the need to protect their process, their right to decide, their objectives, etc., they become adversaries with the other business silos. They don't communicate, coordinate, or cooperate. Instead, they vie for resources, attention, and authority—and the battle is on.

I had one client who told me that his biggest challenge was that he couldn't get his executive leadership team to break down the silos so they could work together. They were entrenched in doing their own thing and being the best at doing things their way. So we started a high-level Trusted Leader process and built a business nozzle using the Partnering Approach. It took time, but slowly the silos began to pass information between each other. Then ideas were shared, and they finally began to coordinate. They talked about how they affected each other's ability to perform and co-created better ways, together. I have learned that you can never get rid of the silos, but you can at least drill some holes in the silos so there is flow between them. But this can't happen without a Trusted Leader that your people will follow.

Tap into the Collective Wisdom

One of the greatest gifts of Trusted Leadership is that you will be able to tap into the collective wisdom of your team and business. I have learned over the years to completely trust that there is a collective wisdom in a team. It could be a project team, a division's team, a joint-venture team, an executive team, or a board of directors. If you, as the

Trusted Leader, can master the skills of creating a high-trust environment and use the Partnering Approach to create an event where people can openly share their ideas and concerns, you will find that your employees will create things that you probably thought were impossible. You won't make mistakes that derail you and your business. The ideas that will emerge from your team might be big or small, but the fact that the team created the idea means they will own it and make it happen.

I recall one team back in the early 2000s that was so excited when I came to facilitate their partnering workshop. They said, "you've got to come out and see what our field leader has done to his truck. He has created ways to save the entire team time and money." So I went out and they opened the door to his truck. Inside, on the passenger side, one of those stadium seats was turned upside down and strapped onto the seat. On the top, where someone would normally sit, there was a platform that held a laptop computer. Underneath, resting on the car seat, was an all-in-one machine: a printer, scanner, fax, and copier that had infrared capability (this is how things were sent wirelessly to a printer before Bluetooth). A power source was on the floor. There was also a hot spot, which supported up to five different devices, so the team could hold their meetings around the front of the truck. They could email right from the hot spot, or they could point their computer at the all-in-one and it would print, make copies for everyone, scan documents, and fax items off.

This team had committed to saving money, and they met their goal in the first season. But they wanted to continue saving during the second season. The team had spent $60K in the first year for testing, so the field leader installed a $600 measuring device in his truck and did the measuring himself—and the team saved that money too. He had a few other devices as well. The team was so excited that they had created a way to be very efficient and effective, even when working in a highly remote area.

Your team can create small things and big things. But it takes a Trusted Leader to create the level of trust required for creativity to occur. The collective wisdom is tapped into in this atmosphere—you can count on it! Because of the team in this example's collective wisdom, their project was improved. I love when I hear comments on the Trusted Leadership Scorecard about how a project or business is better because the team came together. This leads to the growth of the individuals and organizations involved. Your team's collective wisdom is the path for your business' sustainable competitive advantage.

Declare Your Interdependence

Imagine you are in a room filled with 30 people. Fifteen people are on the right side of the room and 15 are on the left side. Get their attention and tell them all that everyone is going to do a breathing exercise.

Ok. Everyone on the right side, you absolutely believe that inhaling is the most important part of breathing. It is only by inhaling that you get the oxygen needed for your cells and brain and this allows you to move and think. Of course, inhaling is most important!

Everyone on the left side, you believe that inhaling is fine, but that exhaling is absolutely the most important. What about all the carbon dioxide that builds up and poisons your body. There is no doubt. Exhaling is the most important!

Now, everyone on the right side is ONLY going to inhale. Everyone on the left side is ONLY going to exhale. Ready. Set. Go.

What do you think happened? Yep, the people on the right side could only <u>inhale</u> for so long before their lungs were full, and the carbon dioxide began to build up. They may have felt a bit light-headed. They just *had* to exhale. What about the people on the left side, the *exhalers*? They could only exhale for so long before their lungs and body began to crave oxygen. They may too have felt a bit light-headed. They just *had* to inhale.

Breathing is, of course, an interdependent system. You need both inhaling and exhaling to succeed. Your business and the world economy have also become interdependent. Your business does not exist in a vacuum. In an interdependent world, it is essential that we all let go of the fear-based Feared Leader and move towards Trusted Leadership. Interdependent relationships are important because each part's success is tied to the other's. So there is only win/win or lose/lose. Nothing else is possible in an interdependent relationship.

Think about the global economy. If the COVID-19 pandemic did anything, it proved to us how interdependent we are. Look at the spread of the virus—it is such a dramatic demonstration how connected we are. Look at how the flow of goods and services was totally disrupted, demonstrating how we are all interdependent. And as artificial intelligence moves forward and we evolve into digital organizations, we are becoming more and more interdependent. Marco Iansiti and Karim R. Lakhani explain in their book *Competing in the Age of AI:*

The new kinds of operating models characterizing firms in the age of AI are binding us together across industries, countries, markets and political affiliations. The many resulting interdependencies have become much too important to ignore and are motivating the need for a new kind of collective wisdom.

That is exactly what you can achieve with Trusted Leadership that uses the Partnering Approach.

I think we should really define this as the Age of Interdependence. When you truly understand and accept that your fates are tied to one another, you are going to make different decisions than if you believe you are on an island. The synergies that are possible when you use the Partnering Approach are so exciting to see. You can get $1 + 1$ to equal 16, or 64, or 6400. The only limits are the imagination of your team and how much you drive out and eliminate a sense of fear.

One Saturday morning my phone rang. It was the leader of the Department of Transportation (DOT). He told me that the almost billion dollars in federal funding allocated for rebuilding a major freeway was going to revert to the federal government in six days if they could not come to agreement. He wanted to use the Partnering Approach.

It had been four years since the freeway had collapsed because of an earthquake. For four years, the DOT had been working on an agreement with the city and local community for the rebuilding of the freeway. Now it seemed that it would not be built.

The strife had been over the local community's wanting the jobs to go to local people. They started monitoring the number of jobs created. Since the state didn't trust the local monitors, they had installed their own monitors. Then the feds felt they also needed their own monitors. So there were monitors to monitor the monitors that monitored the monitors. Soon, naturally, we had three sets of data. Of course, none of the sets matched. There were protests, loud meetings, and storming of buildings.

We decided to gather a group of leaders from each of the different stakeholder groups and use the Partnering Approach to try and co-create a solution. We held a three-day partnering workshop. At first there was a great deal of tension and anger. But gradually, over time, they began to share their perspectives and they actually listened to each other. The group began to see they were locked into an infinity loop and the only way out was to co-create solutions *together*. Over the next three days, this group created seven different incentive programs. The leaders who could authorize each one were in the room! At the end of the three days, this group of adversaries were hugging each other. They stayed together throughout the construction of the project, making sure each stakeholder group understood what was happening, adjusting when things didn't go as planned, and celebrating their success.

The Trusted Leader who had called me on that Saturday morning called me again the day they cut the ribbon to open the freeway. He said that this project would never had been built without the level of trust that was developed between all the stakeholders. Trust can achieve what others believe to be a miracle! It just took a Trusted Leader to make it happen.

In business, we rarely can just go off and do something all on our own and succeed. We need other people to play their part in order for us to succeed. We are intertwined with everyone and every business, potentially on the planet. And that's a good thing, but you have to have a different mindset. You must have a different leadership model to deal with these interdependencies. While artificial intelligence loves complexity, and will chew up data and spit out information, we still need Trusted Leaders who can deal with that information and make decisions in a trusting way that leads to growth, improvement, and progress. I think Trusted Leadership is more sorely needed now than it has ever been. I am hoping that we can get a million Trusted Leaders committed to using the Partnering Approach, so they can tap the collective wisdom. This will allow trust to grow in our businesses and with our partners.

As I mentioned in Chapter 1, at the very first meeting I ever went to for the trade association I led, there was an actual fistfight. I realized that, "Man, these people are really adversaries." Because each one of them was the owner of a construction company and therefore an innately fierce competitor with the others. There was so much competition that even when they came together in their trade association, they were still competing.

In business, even though most of our relationships are highly interdependent, we don't act like they are. Because of our denial, the paradigm and the model that we now use for leadership, working together inside an organization, working with our customers, or working with strategic partners is one where we are way, way too adversarial because we think we can get some kind of competitive advantage. But when win/win or lose/lose is all that is truly available to us, then we need high trust and collaboration. Otherwise, we are actually working against ourselves. A protective mode, in an interdependent relationship, *always* leads to failure for both sides. Too often I see people working to make sure the other side loses more than they do. Hey—this also means you lose!!

When I saw my contractor members fighting, I had an "ah-ha" moment that we needed a different way of working together. I set out to prove to myself, to them, and to the industry, that you could be at least as successful by cooperating and collaborating as you could be by competing and fighting with each other. Today, I know unequivocally that not only can you be as successful, but you can be exponentially more successful. You can achieve things that you never thought were possible and, as a bonus, enjoy your business a whole lot more. Becoming a Trusted Leader has become essential.

In my 35 years of helping leaders build high trust, high performing businesses and teams, my experience is that leadership follows the Pareto principle. It is 80% behavior and 20% know-how. If you are like I am, and you love your business and the people that you serve, then you want to do all you can to be as successful as possible. You want to find a method that will allow you to become a Trusted Leader who creates a high trust business. **That is the Partnering Approach.** Just to remind you of what I said in the introduction, the definitions of a Trusted Leader and the Partnering Approach are:

A **TRUSTED LEADER** is someone who knows that his/her primary role is to develop and maintain an atmosphere of trust with the employees, customers, and vendors. It is only in this kind of atmosphere that your business or team can co-create extraordinary results.

THE PARTNERING APPROACH is a two-step business paradigm that sets up the intentions and the mindset needed to create a high-trust business culture. The intentions help you think like a trusted leader and the mindset values helps to create the behaviors needed in a high-trust culture.

There are two elements to the Partnering Approach:

1. Ten Partnering Principles that create *Partnering Intentions*. This entails how you act as a leader.

2. Six Partnering Values that create a *Partnering Culture*. This involves what you believe in and creates the norms for your business.

We will go in depth on the Partnering Principles and Partnering Values in the next chapters. First, let's continue to explore more about trust.

Becoming A TRUSTED LEADER

Trusted Leaders use the Partnering Approach to build a high-trust atmosphere. But there is a hierarchy to trust. And it starts with you trusting yourself!

You must trust in your own abilities first before you can inspire others to follow. If you feel you are not as capable as you'd like, then it is up to you to gain the knowledge and confidence that will allow you to trust in your own success. This is your critical path to success.

The next level in the hierarchy is your trust in another person and your ability to develop a good relationship with that person. Your ability to be open to another person's needs, thoughts, and ideas is the next step to building your success as a Trusted Leader.

FIGURE 5: Trust Hierarchy

The ability to develop trust when working with a team or group is the next rung on the ladder of trust. Can you take a group of people and build them into an energetic, cohesive team that is excited about working together to accomplish an objective?

Even more complex yet is your ability to influence and develop trust throughout your business' entire organization. This is where you can influence the overall culture and values that drive the organization so that it can foster trust as its foundation.

The most complex situation for developing trust is when there are multiple organizations who must work together. How able are you to develop an atmosphere of trust between divergent interests? Can you inspire the different organizations to find win/win outcomes to the problems that they face?

It takes practice and experience to learn how to develop trust at all these levels. It is a must in today's complex, ever-changing business environment. It is best to start at the pinnacle, self, and then work down from there. Over time, you will gain in your abilities and confidence. For example, a leader that is feeling that he/she can't trust his/her subordinates might take a close look at what kind of atmosphere are they creating, and how their people are reacting.

I have a friend whose business is growing and scaling very quickly. Her team is overwhelmed, tired, frustrated, and sensitive. These are normal growing pains when you scale quickly. How the leader responds to their behavior makes all the difference. As the leader, do you join the team in their downward spiral of exhaustion with equal hostility, or recognize that your team needs relief, and that you are lacking the systems and capacity needed for continued growth? If the leader focuses on providing relief, systems, and capacity, she will find that people will follow her as their leader. Respond as a fearful leader who feels things are out of control, and you will put gas on their fire.

When you can develop and maintain trust at all levels of the hierarchy, there really is NO problem or situation that can arise that you cannot deal with effectively. Use the Partnering Approach to guide you as you move through the Trust Hierarchy.

CHAPTER 4:
Use the Ten Partnering Principles to Create Trusted Leader Intentions

Success is predictable.

BRIAN TRACY

Part one of the Partnering Approach is using the ten Partnering Principles. Over the past 35 years, I've discovered that leaders who embrace the following ten Partnering Principles are able to create the intentions and mindset that create an atmosphere where trust grows.

Your brain is a miraculous biocomputer. Just like with any computer, garbage in = garbage out. If you fill your mind with the things your fear, then that will be your experience in your business. If you fill your mind with what you want, then that will be your experience in your business. It is your choice. Most people don't realize how they are the creators of their own experiences, so they are very lax about what they allow into their minds. Unfortunately, the result is often a life, and a business, filled with frustration, anguish, and helplessness.

If you don't like what is happening in your business, then think again. If your business today isn't what you want it to be, you can change it. If you have problems you don't want to have, then resolve them. Many opportunities come disguised as problems. It all starts with your intentions and mindset. Your people respond to your intentions and to the atmosphere that you create with your mindset. You have total control. Remember, no one has control over your intentions and mindset but you. Your mind is like a muscle that needs exercise. You will need to work at creating the mindset that serves you and your business. My truest wish for you is that you will embrace the ten Partnering Principles to create a trust mindset and atmosphere that have proven to create extraordinary outcomes. I can't wait to hear from you to find out what you and your team are able to co-create!

THE TEN PRINCIPLES OF THE PARTNERING APPROACH

PRINCIPLE #1: Fear Is the Enemy of Trust

As I've mentioned before, fear and trust cannot coexist. Just as when you light a candle in a dark room, the darkness disappears, so too does fear disappear when you fill your business with trust. When you were a child, were you afraid there was a boogeyman under your bed, or in your closet? Fear can be created in your mind, just as trust can be. As a Trusted Leader, your job is to drive out the fear that exists in your business.

The underpinning of trust is being committed to *being fair* in every circumstance. People get hurt and angry when they feel they have been treated unfairly. Whenever you, your employees, or your customers feel things are unfair, fear isn't far behind. People naturally become defensive. This adversarial situation only sets you up for a battle and to see each other as "opponents," working against each other. Trusted Leadership asks that you see each other as *partners*. That you don't let fear stop you from diving in and looking around at what people are telling you. As a result, you should always talk about what is a fair way to deal with every issue, and your reputation for being fair and reasonable will make people trust you as a leader.

One morning, I got a call that picketers were surrounding many of our contractor members' offices. One of the plumber's locals had decided to strike for much higher wages. In fact, they wanted almost four times the wage increase that all the other locals had already agreed upon. I also got a call from the head (business manager) of the plumbers' union district council, to which all the locals belonged. The business manager asked me not to approve an increase for the striking local union. I said of course, because this would have been totally unfair to the rest of the locals and to our members. The strike went on for over a year, with posturing, threats, and picketing.

Eventually, we were able to create a solution that gave the leader of this local union a way to save face and become a hero in the plumbers' district council. We created a new work category and gave that category the high wage, but we wrote it out in a manner that essentially no one could ever get into that category. All the plumbers felt this was a great solution because the other locals had already settled for a small increase and were very angry at this local's leader for breaking ranks. The leader of the striking local could save face and show his people that he did well for them. We also developed a new second tier wage rate so the plumbers could be more competitive with the nonunion workers that were taking a great deal of their market share. This made the leader of the striking local a hero to his people, and also made the other locals happy. This ended the year-long strike. When the NLRB wanted information on what occurred during the strike, the leader of the striking local came to me and asked for my notes to share with them, because he knew my notes would be "right and fair." This is just one story of where fairness sets you apart as a Trusted

Leader. All the other Partnering Principles will also help you drive out fear.

PRINCIPLE #2: Really Care

There is an old adage that says: people don't care until they know that you care. I believe this is as true today as ever, and your business, people, customers, and vendors all need to know that, as a leader, you care, truly care about them, your business, and your mutual success. In this day and age, we often hear that "it's just business, it isn't personal," as business leaders do horrible things to their competitors, employees, and customers. After all, business leaders are supposed to just look out for themselves and their business.

This philosophy also plays out in our news headlines. I recall a story many years ago about a young woman who was beaten to death outside of an apartment house in New York. People listened to her screams and watched her being beaten to death—but no one did anything to stop it. People all over the country were shocked that this could happen. When witnesses were asked why they did nothing, they all said that they were afraid to get involved. I believe we are becoming a nation, and world, that is too often afraid to care about our fellow man. This is one of the reasons why there are so many injustices. Fear keeps us from caring. But, if we cared, truly cared, everything would change. Business is seen as a place where, if I do something that kills your business, well, it isn't personal! And everyone is just supposed to be OK with that?

In the association (of fierce competitors) that I ran, they didn't care about each other at first. They rather hated each other. I see the same thing on projects and within businesses and even within business units and partnerships. They have no regard for one another and see each other as "the enemy." What I've learned is that caring is paradoxical, in that, *by giving up your own self-interest to care and listen to another, and by doing what is fair and good for all concerned, you will get your own needs met.* We have proved it time and time again.

Caring cannot be faked. You must truly care, or people will see right through you. But if you do care in your heart, then caring can never be ignored. People will be drawn to you and follow you. They will stand up and help you because they know that you truly care about them and others. There is nothing in business that is mightier than a committed leader who sincerely cares.

PRINCIPLE #3: People Don't Argue with What They Help to Create

One lesson I've learned is that if you want anyone to buy in and follow through with an initiative that is important to you and your business, then you should create a forum where they help to create what is going to be done. You could be Albert Einstein, Martin Luther King, Jr., Abraham Lincoln, and Mother Theresa all rolled into one awesome leader and still people will fight you if they are not a part of creating the solution, idea, or path forward. The cornerstone of the Partnering Approach is to give people a forum for listening, understanding, and, together, co-creating. The level of commitment and enthusiasm people have can truly do miracles.

I recall working with 75 different stakeholders on an environmental assessment. We had representatives in our partnering process from each of the stakeholder groups, from environmental non-profits; regulatory agencies; local, state, and federal governments; passengers; airlines; airports;

even surfers—everyone who had a stake in the decisions that were to be made. The Partnering Approached included a process for each of the groups to better understand their needs and desires. They got to know each other's, organizations, and as people. They were able to learn from one another. The process allowed everyone to co-create the criteria by which the project would be assessed. Each step of the process, they co-created the options, discussed, prioritized, and analyzed each one. Then they selected three options. In the end, to everyone's amazement, they were all able to agree upon the same option—this was amazing, because at the start, several of the group members swore that they would never agree to anything! By working together to co-create what worked for everyone, they were able to do the impossible.

This process (criteria creation) normally would have taken at least five years, instead of the one year we spent. The likelihood of creating agreed-upon options was about as high as being struck by lightning for the second time. When people feel included and empowered to develop answers, solutions, and ideas, with others involved, they buy-in to what the group creates because they understand why this was the answer. They vet each perspective and have their say. They feel listened to and appreciated. Next time you need real buy-in from your team, create an event that is a forum for everyone to co-create the answers.

PRINCIPLE #4: There Is Collective Wisdom in a Team

The Latin phrase *E Pluribus Unum* means "out of many comes one" or "from many to one." In 1776, our Founding Fathers selected this phrase as the principle upon which the United States is based. This phrase acknowledges that there is *collective wisdom* in a group of people who come together.

FIGURE 6: U. S. Seal

I have learned to completely trust that there is collective wisdom in a business, team, or organization. The job of the Trusted Leader is to tap into the collective wisdom. With this wisdom you will be able to do things that you never thought were possible.

When I am faced with a challenge, I see it from my own perspective. It is my perspective; it must be right. But when I am willing to listen to your perspective, I begin to see that there are more facets to the challenge (or opportunity) than I saw from my perspective. If you listen to ten more people's perspectives, you will begin to see how challenges and opportunities are not one dimensional; rather, they are multidimensional, and you will see many commonalities. Can you imagine trying to create the best strategy for a challenge or opportunity when you only have a small part of the full picture? We do it all the time. We assume that our perspective is right and that yours, if it differs, is wrong. We spend all our time trying to convince others that our perspective is right, when in fact both perspectives are right, from each person's point of view. If I am in my office and you are 20,000 feet above looking down at my office, what you see looks very different from what I see. Are you wrong? Am I wrong?

If you can learn to trust that there is a collective wisdom, you will be amazed how people can cull out the core issues or create opportunities that no one in the room ever would have thought of on their own. One client of mine had a team that was not talking to each other. They were not telling each other the "bad news." Everyone just wanted to do his or her job and not get blamed for the delayed opening of the two million square foot building. Their leader brought them all together and told them that they needed to figure out what was creating the delay. One by one, they spoke up, and together they developed a list of the six most critical items that were needed for a successful opening. They knew that if they all stayed focused on these six things over the next two months, that they would successfully open on time. That is exactly what they did.

Your leadership is the critical element. I know leaders who say they believe in creating a high-trust atmosphere, and yet are not willing to delegate anything to their people. Just remember, whenever you are faced with a problem, challenge, risk, or opportunity and there are several people involved, that there is collective wisdom available to you that will provide you with the insight to make the best decisions.

PRINCIPLE #5: Refuse to Be an Adversary

What is an adversary? It is someone you see as your opponent. How do you see someone in your own business as your opponent? Well, it happens in an instant, in your mind. When someone is talking to you, and you hear this little inner voice saying, "that's not true," "that isn't what happened," "I'm never going to do that," or anything similar. You've just become an adversary to that person.

Your mind will move swiftly to protect you, to look for ways to keep you safe. Is your mind focused on understanding, resolving, or creating? NO! Your mind is busy creating your defense, your rebuttal to prove that your opponent is wrong and that you are right! The ironic thing that I've learned over the past 35 years of working with leaders is that, as soon as your mind flips into adversarial mode, you've lost! You are now part of the problem, and you have hijacked your mind from being able to create solutions or opportunities. The entire conversation will be focused on winning—or at least, not losing. Meanwhile, the issue that started it all is still there, but now no one is focused on resolving the issue.

I started talking to the leaders of a large water treatment project. I had been asked to come help the team. The contractor and the owner had their trailers on site, side by side. But the job was so contentious that both trailers were locked to keep the other team out. Both the owner and contractor teams spent their days emailing threats back and forth. Communication was loud, harsh, and unproductive. In preparation for my kick-off meeting, I interviewed the leaders. I learned that for the two weeks before the partnering workshop, things were "much improved"—simply because they completely stopped talking to each other! I also learned that at the very first project meeting, one of the leaders had felt slighted. Since that meeting, the conflict had continued to play out. Now the project was six months behind schedule and millions of dollars over budget. It happens that fast. Neither side realized that the snowballing conflict was from the leader's hurt feelings. After a sincere apology and co-creating solutions to improve the outcome of their project, the teams started moving forward, together!

Refuse to be an adversary—no matter what!! Over the years, I have been shot at, had my life threatened twice, had to leave town with my family, and had my phone tapped. But no one ever knew these things were going on, because I acted as if I had the relationships and results that I wanted, and I refused to become an adversary.

PRINCIPLE #6: Set Partnering Ground Rules

Setting ground rules for your partnering meetings, where you are going to explore ideas or solutions, is a great way to help create a safe environment for people to talk openly and honestly. As I mentioned before, this is what creates the atmosphere that allows for creativity and innovation to emerge. And of course, your people won't argue with what they create; they will buy in and be committed to following through. Here is an example of some Partnering Approach Ground Rules:

- Everyone is created equal—we are one team
- This is an opportunity to listen to and understand each other
- There are no dumb ideas or dumb questions
- Focus on the issue/opportunity and not on personalities—we accept people as they are
- Now is the time for open, honest communication

- Judgments are not allowed—silence your inner judge and listen

Once you and your team get used to creating a high-trust atmosphere, allow your team to co-create their own *ground rules.*

Some boards, partnerships, or leadership teams might want to develop some governance ground rules for how they are going to operate as a high-trust, high-performing leadership team. These ground rules differ, as they will include how the leaders make decisions—by majority or by shares, ownership percentage, etc. They will want ground rules for each type of meeting they hold, including things like attendance at these meetings. Who runs the meetings, sets up the agenda, and writes the notes? By creating some governance ground rules that are designed to create a high-trust atmosphere, you can prevent many of the leadership dysfunctions that I see in businesses. Of course, the leadership dysfunctions trickle down to all of the employees in the business. Examples of some Governance Ground Rules are:

- One vote per person—a simple majority passes
- Attendance is required, no substitutes
- You may miss one meeting per year
- Senior leadership positions are a shared decision
- Once a decision is made, even if it isn't what you wanted, you own the decision
- We are open, honest, and transparent with what is going on with the business
- We tell our employees everything so they can be part of the solutions and ideas

One last thing about ground rules. It is important for you, as the Trusted Leader, to provide context to your employees, so they understand the task at hand, how it affects the business, and what you specifically need from them. Share a story and your vision. Your people can't create without understanding what you need and why.

PRINCIPLE #7: To Improve Communication, Stop Talking and Ask Good Questions

As I mentioned in Chapter 2, I asked 134 different project teams to think about the very best project they had ever been on in their careers. Then I asked them to think about the very worst project they had every been on. Over 95% said that communication was the key to success. Ninety-eight percent said poor communication was what derailed them.

In other words, communication is pretty darn important. And yes, it is a direct indicator of the level of trust. But for most of us, we think of communication as telling our side or story, then listening with our brain running to make sure we comment or rebut what is said to us. This pattern of conversation undermines your ability to communicate. Communication requires a sender and a receiver. Even though we are far more skilled at being senders, I've learned that when we stop talking and start listening, we can improve communication by around 50%. This is especially true if you are the leader. Because you are the one with the authority over people, they will defer to you, and you may think they understand and agree, but far too often that is the opposite of what is going on.

I was asked to help a large building project that wasn't going well. It was a unique project in that it was a city hall that had an historic building attached to where they were adding on a large modern building. The city hired a developer to build the new building and completely renovate the historic section. Then, once completed, the building was to be sold to the city. It was complicated. There were problems with the inspection. There were problems with the design. There were problems with decision making. It got worse as time went on.

When I interviewed all the parties involved, for our partnering workshop, I found out that some of the people on the team didn't know that this was a developer project being done for the city, and that it was being done using a joint design-builder. This was very different from what they were used to. This project had a different set of roles and responsibilities. They had been acting as if it was just a regular low-bid project. The disconnect on roles and responsibilities played out every day. Even when I explained to the leader that this was what I had heard, they denied that that could be the case. It wasn't until the people on the team explored roles and responsibilities that they all realized they were not on the same page. Misaligned roles and responsibilities happen often within businesses and play out for months, sometimes years, because neither side knows it is happening—they just think people are being difficult.

Listening pays off. Reading between the lines to what people are really trying to tell you also pays off. Practicing empathy so you really can hear what people need is a wonderful skill that anyone can practice and learn. Empathy is the ability to enter someone's world and feel what they feel, so that you understand on an emotional level what it is like to be them. When you can do this, you understand what is needed to solve the problems that you face. Empathy is a gift you can give to anyone. It is a gift because one of our greatest needs as human beings is to be known and understood, and to be accepted anyway. This is true for you, your employees, and your customers.

While listening will get you a 50% improvement, it is also important to probe so you can learn more. You have got to ask good questions, so you get good answers.

When you pose to others the questions that need to be answered, you are opening up the possibility of empathy, really understanding the problem, understanding the different points of view, and co-creating answers to the questions posed. Asking questions is one of the most powerful tools you can use to grow trust.

If you ask people the burning questions that need to be answered, you will get answers that will give everyone what they need. For example, I conducted a trust building session for a large city. Their team consists of outside consultants, and city employees from different departments within the city. The team had been working together for over a year and trust, communication, and teamwork had continued to decline.

The city employees resented that outside consultants were brought in. The outside consultants didn't understand the city's processes and procedures, and felt like second class citizens. The different city departments had been competing with each other for over 30 years. These factors had created a dysfunctional team that worked at cross-purposes. In our trust-building session, we focused on answering the question "how can we work together more effectively?" We concentrated on what working together as a team would look like. We discussed who would do what. We evaluated what barriers existed to working together by convening a cross-functional group to share where communication and conflict were occurring, as well as where there was poor performance. At the end of the day, we had an open dialogue on some of the frustrations people had been feeling, and set goals and commitments to overcome them. The leader and various team members committed to helping to remove the barriers. It would not be easy for them to build trust, but now they had a road map.

In the example above, we focused the entire day on answering one question: "How can we work together more effectively?" Working together as a team is what everyone knew they needed—they just weren't sure how to get there. Everything we did helped us to answer that one question.

What do you think our outcome would have been if we had posed the question, "what is wrong with this team and its leadership?" Or "why isn't this team performing as it should be?" In both of these questions, we are focusing on the problem and not on what needs to happen in order for everyone on this team to be successful. Good questions always focus on what you *want*, and *not* on what you don't want.

If you were to ask yourself, "where do I want to be in five years?" what would you answer? What if you asked yourself, "what do I need to do in order to get there?" How about, "what are the steps I need to take over the next 12 months to get where I want to be in five years?" These are all good questions. They lead you to understand what the solutions are. If instead you had asked yourself, "why am I not achieving what I want?" what would you have answered? Or if you had asked yourself, "where have I gone wrong?" or "who is to blame for this situation?" These are not good questions, because they don't help you understand the steps to solving the underlying problem.

PRINCIPLE #8: It's Never the Challenges You Face That Determine Your Success or Failure

One thing I've learned after working with over 4,000 different teams is it is *never* the number or size of the challenges that determines if you succeed or fail, but rather how well your team comes together to address the challenges. Every day in business, you face challenges and opportunities. I've seen leaders and their team obstructed by what seem to be insurmountable challenges, and still they came together and accomplished what people thought to be impossible. I've seen teams that could literally not agree on the measurement of a square or the time of day to hold a meeting.

As the leader, you want your team to create a history of successfully dealing with challenges (or opportunities). Use the ten Partnering Principles to guide you. Start with small issues and then bring on larger ones. The idea is that once the team has true confidence that they know how to work together to resolve the challenges the business faces, there won't be any issue, of any size, that they can't tackle together. They may actually learn that inside every problem lies an opportunity and look forward to the challenge.

Some time back, I worked on two identical highway projects that were located side by side. They had different teams, but they had the same scope and problems. Not long after starting, both teams ran into a great deal of hazardous materials on their respective projects. One team brought in experts and did a lot of testing to identify their options. They selected the best option and implemented it right away. The other team, decided to write and email each other official letters stating their position, telling the other team members how this was not "my" problem and explaining why they were not responsible. There was a total of 1,500 such letters. They had to hire extra people just to answer the letters that were emailing back and forth.

The team that worked to understand and tackle the problem, found their best solution was to shut down the project for six months to allow for remediation, then started back up afterwards. The team that looked to pass the blame for the problem was delayed two years. The project that addressed the issue was completed a year before their next-door project, with half the cost. The number of hours to complete the project by the letter-writing team was for both the contractor and owner teams many times more. Same problems. But very different approaches. And more importantly, very different outcomes. What about for you and your business? Are you addressing issues together and working out the best path forward?

I shared this story once in a partnering workshop for a very large project. I was told that this was nothing new because this team could not even agree on the day and time to hold their progress meetings. These Partnering Principles are here to help you and your team work together to grow and scale your business, so you can provide the best product or service of anyone in your sector. Not as a strong leader, but as a Trusted Leader, with your trusted team! Then you will become a trusted business!

PRINCIPLE #9: There Is Energy in Conflict

I see how leaders are conflict adverse all the time. They put off having the hard conversations. They talk behind people's backs because of their discomfort, or just ignore problems that can sink the business because they don't want to deal with the people involved.

Please know that there is energy in conflict that can be unleashed to create solutions and ideas for transforming the situation. I actually get excited when I have a conflict to resolve, because I know that no one wants to be in disagreement (well, attorneys might be the exception), so when they can see how they can co-create a great solution, it really ramps up the energy and level of commitment.

I studied the martial art Aikido. Aikido has no offensive moves, only defensive moves. It is designed to neutralize the attacker without harming them. You use the attacker's own energy to neutralize them. Once neutralized, you can help the attacker see a new direction. This is exactly how it works when dealing with conflict. Don't be afraid of it. Dive in and look around. See what you learn, what people need. Try to create ways to help everyone get there. Look for ways to use the conflict's energy to transform it into a lasting and creative solution!

I recall working with a firm where the board of directors voted to close the business. After three years of turmoil, the three original owners were ready to call it quits and close the doors. The three new partners, who had been brought in to carry on when the original owners retired, were disappointed, but agreed that things were not working.

After many days of partnering dialogue, the original owners agreed that one of the three new partners was someone they trusted to be their heir. They felt that this man was like a son to them. His father had been one of the original owners but had passed away shortly after starting the firm. The two younger partners disagreed with the direction that the new heir wanted to take the firm. Once they understood that he was selected to be the heir, they decided it was time for them to leave, but they wanted financial restitution.

In the partnership agreement, the calculation for price per share was spelled out. The three original owners wanted to do what was right and fair, so they immediately paid them in total. I know the departing partners felt they had been treated well, because at different times both called me and thanked me for helping them. Though they were very disappointed, they felt they had been treated fairly and with dignity. The three years of conflict was over. In three years, the business had tripled in size. The conflict helped them to work toward a great solution for everyone involved.

PRINCIPLE #10: Understand All Interests

I am always amazed how people feel they must protect themselves from others. This need for protection often sets us up to fail, especially if we are interdependent, like I talked about in Chapter 3. If you are a leader with a team that wants customers, you are all interdependent! The leader needs the team in order to produce the product or service to sell. The team needs the leader to provide a living for them and their families, along with meaningful work. This is a highly interdependent relationship. But still leaders and their teams usually don't realize how they are undermining themselves by thinking they need to protect themselves from each other.

FIGURE 7: Understanding Interests

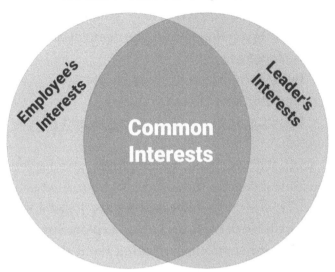

Let's explore the leader's and employee's interests in working for your business.

The employee's interests might include:
- Earning a paycheck and other benefits
- Contributing to the success of the business
- Opportunity to grow with the business
- Friendships and camaraderie
- A place to use your gifts
- Recognition for your contributions
- Increasing market share and brand recognition

The business leader's interests might include:
- Earning a good living and creating something worthwhile
- Having a successful business
- Opportunity to grow the business and your employees

- Friendships and close relationships with people who are helping you create your dream
- Making a difference for your employees and customers
- Being recognized for your success and contributions in your industry
- Growing your business margins and profits

If you look at these lists, the employee and leader interests are almost exactly the same!! All your interests are in common! This is what interdependence looks like. Good decisions are built of trust, and if you explore your interests, you will develop a stronger trusting bond that will allow you to make better decisions.

I've done this exercise dozens of times. I ask each "side" to write down all the things they need to be successful. Then they read their lists to each other. I then ask them what interests they have in common. They are always flabbergasted when everyone writes down the exact same things!!

This is a great exercise for you to use anytime you want to really explore what it takes for success when there is resistance and fear. Jump in and look around, explore what each of you needs to be successful. You will be amazed how similar it is if you are in a relationship, like employee/employer, partners, division leader, board members, etc.

CHAPTER 5:
Create a Trusted Leader Mindset
Using the Six Partnering Values

*Leadership is 80% behavior
and 20% know-how.*

SUE DYER

FIGURE 8: The Trusted Leadership Value Chain

The Trusted Leadership Value Chain

Alignment | Cohesion | Collective Wisdom | Innovation | Momentum | EBO Extraordinary Business Outcomes

Your Company Culture Rules Your People

Part 2 of the Partnering Approach is using the six partnering values. As a Trusted Leader using the Partnering Approach, you are working to align your entire team behind a common purpose. The Trusted Leadership Value Chain shows how this plays out. You lead your team to work together to achieve alignment behind a focus. Alignment leads to a sense of cohesion and shared purpose. This allows for the team to tap into the collective wisdom of their fellow team members. Innovative ideas emerge that are better than what otherwise would be possible. With the excitement of their creation, as these are implemented, the team gains more and more momentum. Ultimately, this results in achieving Extraordinary Business Outcomes (EBO)!

As the Trusted Leader, it is your job to instill your business with the Partnering Values. This will create a high-trust culture. Culture is based on what you value—the values that you bring with you to your business. What you value plays out in your people and how they do things. So the question to ask yourself is, what are the values you need to create in yourself, in your people, and in your business, in order to create this high-trust culture?

Your company culture rules your people. I am going to say that again. Your culture rules your people. I am sure that you have procedures and processes, and these are a part of your culture. Walk into a business, any business, and sit there for five or ten minutes and listen to how people talk, how they deal with each other, and you can begin to feel the culture. Norms are so powerful that if you create the norms that you want, people adopt those norms. And norms are what define a culture.

For example, maybe I'm an atheist and I'm going to go to dinner with a group of my dear friends, several of whom are very religious. So, at the dinner table they hold hands and each person says a prayer. What am I going to do? There is a very high probability that I'm going to hold hands and say a prayer. That's the power of norms. Norms tell us what's the right thing to do in a situation. And creating the norms for your business, based on Partnering Values, is how you lead your people. How do you create the atmosphere that allows for them to thrive and teach you things?

Many business leaders ask me, "how do I know what my culture is?" Your culture exists in your policies, practices, and processes. So, look at your policies. What do they say you value? What about your practices? Practices are the ways you do things that aren't written down. And your processes and procedures, what are they?

For one organization, we started with identifying the barriers to trust. They came up with dozens of policies that worked against the development of trust. One policy was that if something was in the specification/contract, then the project leader must enforce that requirement, even if it is unfair. This policy created hundreds of claims each year. It didn't foster trust or communication. When the chief engineer changed this policy and told his leaders that their job was to be fair, it shifted everything and allowed for open dialogue and problem solving to figure out what was fair, given the circumstances. (Ultimately this policy change saved them millions of dollars.)

In another instance, I started working with the new leader of a large public organization. His predecessor was a command and control person (Feared Leader), so the executive team was used to things getting political and to taking orders. The new leader wanted to create a high-trust culture. You can imagine how the policies, practices, and processes that existed with the entire team had to be shifted and changed. One thing that really stood out was the practice of not meeting.

The executive leaders, each of which headed up a department, never met (yes, another organization where the leadership team did not come together). Issues and problems just lingered and festered. People were frustrated that they could not solve the problems that they faced each day.

Fear was rampant. Each department protected their silo and their people. The new leader created an executive steering committee that brought the leaders of each department together to steer. Your company's culture rules your people and determines what is possible. For this group, they have become a strong, smart team that is growing the organization to become extraordinary in their market.

If you embrace becoming a Trusted Leader and having a high-trust culture, but your policies, practices, and processes are inconsistent with the Partnering Values, then you have a problem. Because these inconsistencies will create entropy. There will be misalignment. People won't trust you. They won't believe you, and they'll be fearful.

FIGURE 9: Values – Attitudes – Behaviors

It is important to understand how values create your culture. And how those values determine the behavior or your people. I am often asked by leaders, "I want to have people behave a certain way. I want them to be motivated. I want them to take ownership of their piece of the work. I want them to be …" *whatever* they want. To change behaviors in people you must back into it, because it starts with your business' values. The values create attitudes, and those attitudes play out in behaviors. So if you ever want to change the behaviors of your people, you have got to start with the values of your business, and you, as the leader, create those values. They exist in your policies, practices, and processes. Change must start with you and the values you want to instill.

If you're a small business, it's not too hard to examine your current business values and create high-trust Partnering Values. I have also seen very large businesses with literally tens of thousands of people work together as a leadership team to co-create new policies, practices, and processes that created a high-trust partnering culture. The larger you are, the greater effort and structure needed. But huge businesses can turn around their culture and become a high-trust, high-functioning organization. It is well worth the effort!

Are You Behaving Your Way to Success? Or Failure?

Behaviors are really what define success, right? Because don't you have to behave your way to success? If you want to be more successful, you've got to have the right behaviors. And you've got to have everybody behaving correctly in order to be successful. That's why norms, values, and leadership are so important. So what values will create your norms for success? The Partnering Values. These are the values that I have discovered over the years from 4,000 different teams, 48,000 executive leaders.

Partnering Values create an atmosphere that allows for partnering to happen, where people work together in cooperation. You, as the Trusted Leader, are the one who sets the values. Use these six Partnering Values, along with the ten Partnering Principles of the Partnering Approach, to create your intentions, mindset, and culture.

THE SIX PARTNERING VALUES

VALUE #1: Trust

Trust, we know, is the pinnacle. Trust is what allows everything else to occur. This book is all about creating high-trust, high-performing businesses. However, I routinely see businesses that just can't seem to make decisions because they don't have enough trust. And this really holds them back.

Trust is the driving force for good decision making. As I've said before, when trust levels are low, people hold back and don't tell each other everything. Confidence, communication, and creativity can't occur, and decisions just don't get made. Low levels of trust also prevent delegating decision making to others. Without trust, teams wait around for *someone* to make the decision, so they can move forward. Yes, you can see the entropy building!

When you are establishing or re-establishing trust, be patient. Some people have high thresholds for trusting because of life experiences where they were hurt. Be trusting and trustworthy, and over time they will begin to believe you—and trust will grow. Start out with little commitments to one another. Then, as you see that each of you has done what you said, trust will grow. Trust is usually a self-fulfilling prophecy. If you give trust, you are likely to get trust in return. When you are distrusting, you are likely to get distrust in return. You have a great deal of control over the level of trust. Once trust is lost, it takes time and patience to regain it. So work to develop and maintain a high level of trust before you have problems.

VALUE #2: Fairness

Next is fairness. Fairness is really the underpinning of trust. Think about it. Usually somebody gets upset and starts to distrust when they think something isn't fair. "I'm not being treated fairly. That's not fair, they got more than I did. I've got more than do you," whatever. They feel that things aren't fair. So fairness is an important thing, as a leader, to always be talking about. If somebody feels something isn't fair, then let's put it on the table and let's talk about it. Let's figure it out.

I've worked with businesses, project teams, and organizations that have been in high conflict. Even so, when they put trust on the table and talk about what's fair, I've yet to have a team not be able to figure it out. We inherently know what's fair. But it still takes a commitment. It is far too easy to feel the need to protect, judge, or blame. Don't. Instead, have a dialogue until you get to what is fair. And then once everyone feels it is fair (such as "Okay, that seems fair," "Don't like it wholly maybe, but that's reasonable," "I can live with that."), we've moved into the realm of trust needed for high performance. You will see the behaviors shift when everyone knows they are going to be treated fairly. People will not longer hold back to see what happens.

VALUE #3: Transparency

Transparency is a key Partnering Value. You've got to be open, honest, and transparent. Tell each other everything—good, bad, and ugly. Identify things in advance, as far out as possible. Tell each other stuff. The more informed everyone can be, the more you are going to be able to become a high-performing team. When you don't tell each other things, people don't know what they don't know. They are making decisions in a vacuum. It's like going to Las Vegas and deciding to play poker, except there are 10 cards missing from the deck, but you don't know which cards are missing, and you didn't even know any were missing, and you just bet the ranch on your hand. You can't do that. You've got to be transparent.

Transparency is an act of trust, especially if you feel that your openness can create a liability for you. You, as the Trusted Leader, must never use the information people share through transparency against them (barring illegal acts). Remember, you are trying to see the full picture and understand what is possible, what is needed, what is going to happen, etc. Only then can you create solutions or come up with ideas that are optimal.

VALUE #4: Respect

You've got to respect people as they are, including their flaws. Have you ever been in a group of people where there's some conflict going on? Maybe someone is feeling like they're not respected. But when people begin to actually listen to each other and learn how extraordinary this person is, or about some skills they have you didn't know about, all of a sudden, the level of respect goes up dramatically. Mutual respect comes from appreciation. Most of us go through life thinking that if a little bit of me is good, then a lot of me would be great! So we judge people that are different from us as bad, when in fact it is those differences that make your team and business more powerful. Because you respect your teammates, you might say, "Oh, they see things differently than I do. Let me listen to them and understand." Or "Oh, I never thought about that. I never looked at it that way. I never realized that was also a part of whatever it is we're trying to do." Listening to each other because you respect each other is pretty magical.

Respect should also be proactive. Since people need to feel appreciated (it's part of being human), make a habit of offering your appreciation. I recall working with an IT department at a large company. Everyone was in cubicles working away. I saw from a distance that several of the cubicles had cards pinned up all over the outside of their cubicle. When I went up and looked at what these were, I found out that the CEO walked the floor every week and when he saw someone doing something he though was great, he handwrote a personal thank you note. There were dozens of thank you notes on the walls of the cubicles. For sure, no one ever threw one of those notes away. In fact, some were framed, hanging inside the cubicles. The power of thank yous and showing your appreciation should not be underestimated.

VALUE #5: Collaboration

Collaboration is the result of creating a high-trust atmosphere. It allows you to tap into the collective wisdom of your team or group. According to the Google Dictionary, the definition of collaboration is "the action of working with someone to produce or create something." Trust creates the potential for three levels of collaboration:

1. Cooperation

2. Collaboration

3. Co-creation

When people come together, they go, "Okay. I think I'm going to *cooperate*. I'm willing to give this a try." When people trust enough to *collaborate*, it is like they are two teams working *together*. They trust enough to brainstorm ideas. When they have built enough trust to *co-create*, they have become one seamless team. You can't tell who "belongs" to whom. They are focused on innovating and creating.

Collaboration takes effort. This is especially true in larger businesses where there is a pull and a tendency to become siloed. As the Trusted Leader, you must continuously work against people pulling away into separate tribes. My experience is that a structured collaborative process gives your business a forum for everyone to come together and collaborate around an opportunity, strategy, or issue. Then, everyone who originally committed to what was created (that they helped to create) owns it and will help implement it.

VALUE #6: Helpfulness

Your business will have challenges, but they will be far easier to deal with if everyone values being helpful. Helpfulness is being of service. It is offering to be useful to others. Having a business composed of people who are in service to their colleagues, customers, and community causes your business to thrive.

I heard a story from a negotiator at a very large computer company who was on a team of seven charged with negotiating a deal with an Asian company overseas. They all arrived on day one in their blue suits and red ties. They sat on the floor while an older woman served them tea. This continued each day for two weeks. The team had been curious how a decision might be made, but never said anything. They continued meeting and talking, but with no conclusion. Finally, at the end of the second week, one of the IT team blurted out, "Who is the decision maker here, anyway?" That is when they learned that it was the older woman who had been serving them. It turned out that she was so powerful that she needed to show her respect by *being of service.*

How do you lead your business? Are you "of service" to your people? To your customers? I've found being helpful to be a wonderful way to show people that you truly care and don't think you are above them. It breaks down the barriers that can otherwise prevent you from becoming a Trusted Leader.

The Atmosphere You Create Defines What Is Possible

This entire book is about developing a Trusted Leader culture by using the Partnering Approach that includes the Partnering Principles to create Trusted Leader intentions, and using the Partnering Values to create a Trusted Leader mindset. The culture, the atmosphere, that *you* create determines what is possible. You need a high-trust culture. Even if you don't feel fully trusting of the other person, unit, or company, you can make the decision to trust. You come to the table to collaborate and explore interests, building on what you have in common. You can create enormous benefits for everyone involved. By now I hope you've realized that you are much more *interdependent* than you ever realized. When you're interdependent, it's really a special relationship. Think about it. If you're interdependent, then when you move forward, *they* have to move forward too. If they don't, you can't either. It really defines what is possible.

In Chapter 2, I talked about wasting energy, or entropy, and the nozzle effect, where you can increase what you achieve by being aligned and focused, so you get more velocity and momentum. I mentioned that I would tell you more about this later. Well, here it is. Years ago, I was part owner of an engineering firm. In that engineering firm, we went into power plants and placed instrumentation throughout the plant. We had proprietary models that we would run data through so we could tell the power plant operator, "Okay, change out these pipes and put in a new value here, and run the turbine at this rate." Then, for the same amount of fuel, the power plant was able to generate ~10% more electricity. It was like putting a nozzle on a hose.

All these concepts have analogies in science: the first law of thermodynamics, second law of thermodynamics, entropy, and chaos theory. Over the years and through thousands of iterations, I've seen that these same concepts work in businesses and for teams. Businesses heat up and take off or get cold and go stale. I've applied this approach to small, medium, large, and mega-sized businesses, teams, and projects. It took me almost 30 years and over 3,000 iterations to create a structured model that provides predictable results.

I did most of my experimentation in my living laboratory (on construction projects), where there are many projects and you can measure your results, adjust your methods, and try again. There has been research done by Michigan State University on the construction partnering model, and it showed a very similar result to the power plants, a cost savings of ~10%, a time savings of ~10%, and an increase in satisfaction of ~10%.

Over the years, I've had projects save as much as 40% of their installed cost (on a $350 million dollar project, that is $140 million dollars). Most of the cost savings came from the team going faster and being smarter. On average, most teams have been able to save around 10% of their total costs, and all that falls to profit. What if you can achieve the same mindset and approach to sales? To production? To distribution? To strategic alliances? To innovating something new? The cumulative effect of multiple 10% improvements is potentially 10 x 10 x 10 … = 100s of percent improvement!

Create Greater Possibilities

If you go to Las Vegas and play blackjack, but you play by the rules for gin rummy, you are playing by the wrong rules! The rules and game you play determine what is possible. Trusted Leadership is a different game and has a different set of rules. Many businesses and industries today are still playing by the old adversarial protection rules. They play the zero-sum game, where one person wins, and one person loses. Why are businesses run this way so often? I believe it is because businesses run on agreements and contracts. The judicial process that governs our businesses is, by design, an adversarial system. When there is a disagreement, two people make a case in front of a third party, and the third party decides who wins and who loses. As you may recall, whenever there's a winner and a loser, that is an adversarial fear-based paradigm, and when you are interdependent, that provides a lose/lose result.

If you look at the political world, like Republicans and Democrats in the United States, it operates under the zero-sum game. Nobody gives anything to anyone without being given something in return. The zero-sum game means that one-plus-one has to equal zero. Think about how many resources you're putting in, to get zero. And we wonder why we don't make progress. By changing the game to Trusted Leadership and the Partnering Approach, cooperating and innovating together, you can get one plus one to equal four or 16. This is what you are working to achieve for your business.

I hear everywhere today—on the news, from politicians, and even on podcasts—how business is a war and business is bad. This view *assumes* that business is a zero-sum game. In other words, for me to get what I want (maximum money), you (my customer) must lose! This belief makes us view what is possible as very limited.

There is little room for creativity, caring, or adding value. I personally *love* business. I experience it as one of the *most* creative forces on the planet. We just have too many leaders who still operate under the old adversarial paradigm. We are far too interdependent for this to work in the long run.

A zero-sum game can be depicted as:

$$1 + 1 = 0$$

When we want something and there is conflict, we are encouraged to "just compromise." Indeed, sometimes compromise is the best solution, but it is not very creative.

When we compromise, we split the difference between two possibilities. While compromise does give us a solution, many times people keep score. "I've compromised twice before; now it is your turn to compromise."

Compromise can be depicted as:

$$1 + 1 = 1\,\tfrac{1}{2}$$

The goal of Trusted Leadership, using the Partnering Approach to do business, is to create a solution that gives everyone what he/she needs. When you give people a specific goal, their minds seek ways to achieve it. When we take the limitations off and allow imaginations to flow, we will be amazed at what can be created.

Creativity can be depicted as:

$$1 + 1 = 3$$

When those involved set aside their differences and begin to really care about each other, they begin to work as a team. They can start to co-create ideas and solutions. This allows them to bounce ideas off one another and push the envelope of what might be possible.

Co-creation can be depicted as:

$$1 + 1 = 30$$

People with an adversarial business paradigm seek to divide the pie among all those involved. Everyone involved with an issue will be working hard at protecting their piece of the pie. From the zero-sum perspective, we need to win in order to protect our piece of the pie—or we lose it all.

The goal of a Trusted Leader, using the Partnering Approach, is to *expand* the pie, so there is more for everyone. We may even come up with a breakthrough along the way—

something that has never been thought of before. As I've said before, there is collective wisdom in a diverse, focused team. They can co-create something that no one ever thought of before, or thought was even possible. They can accomplish amazing things by being open, honest, and creative. That is how businesses can learn and grow and become exponentially better at helping the clients they serve.

Looking at the *Pie of What is Possible* goes something like this:

FIGURE 9A: Zero Sum Game

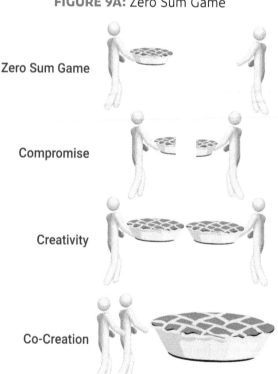

ZERO SUM GAME
You Win or You Lose the Pie

COMPROMISE
We Split the Pie

CREATIVITY
We Expand the Pie for Both

CO-CREATION
We Continue to Expand the Pie Together

I believe that those of you who truly master Trusted Leadership and use the Partnering Approach will understand that a business and team of divergent interests can in fact come together and co-create great designs, solutions, and innovations. You will have learned to co-create solutions to complex, challenging issues. You will be light-years ahead of most business leaders today. Think about all that is lost to the economy, to people who could be helped, and to the overall morale of the country by holding on to the paradigm that business is a zero-sum game.

I hope you will do all you can to try and teach your customers, employees, vendors, colleagues, and associations that business is not a zero-sum game. You can at least explain to them that yours is not!!

CHAPTER 6:
Start Your Journey Along the Leadership Continuum

> *The key to change ...*
> *is to let go of fear.*
>
> ROSANNE CASH

FIGURE 10: The Five Leadership Styles

W e looked at the left side of the Leadership Continuum, at the Feared Leader. We've also looked at he right side, at the Trusted Leader side. But, there are four other leadership styles that make up the Leadership Continuum. Each type is a step along the path toward Trusted Leadership. Let's take a look at all five leadership styles, so you have a feel for each one. No one is a "pure" style. Most of us fluctuate between styles based on the situation. But you most likely have one or two primary styles that you use most of the time. The goal is to continue to move along the continuum until you are using the Trusted Leadership style most of the time. So, let's take a look at them.

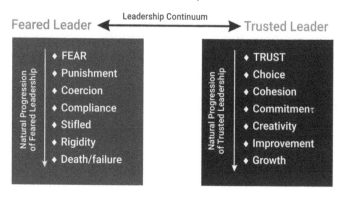

FIGURE 1: Leadership Continuum

THE FIVE LEADERSHIP STYLES

STYLE #1: Feared Leader

If you are a **Feared Leader,** you use fear as your primary team motivator. You've somehow learned that this is what best motivates your people to do their job. Business is a constant struggle. You truly believe that you have everyone's best interest at heart, and you are just trying to make sure everyone succeeds and keeps their jobs. You want to have a highly successful business. You get frustrated when your competitors seem to be gaining on you. So you tighten the reins and push your people harder. Punishment is the way you make people understand that there are consequences to not doing what you ask. You have used coercion to root out the people who are problem makers. You feel compelled to figure out who is to blame.

The result? People in your business do not feel that they can speak up, let alone tell you the truth. They give up and just go along with what you say and wait for their next assignment. Instead of listening to your team members, you usually judge them to be "grumblers." By commanding and controlling, you believe that you can ensure the best possible business outcomes.

You will begin to improve your situation when you can see that your approach is not working and can never work. It is hurting you, your employees, and your overall business. If you don't change, you will fail; it is only a matter of when. You as the leader must be the one to break this vicious cycle.

The best way to start is by using the Partnering Approach, with its Principles and Values (Chapters 4 and 5). You may need a coach or guide to help you and your team see that you can change. It will take time for your team to trust in the change. You will make two steps forward and one backward, but it will happen if you stay fully committed. It will be totally worth it. You will find that your business and life will get a lot easier and much more successful.

I have worked with over 48,000 executive leaders over the past 35 years. For some it took over a decade for them to really learn how to become a Trusted Leader, as opposed to a Feared Leader. And at times, the old Feared Leader can show up briefly. But leaders that learn how to transform into Trusted Leaders typically learn at a deep level. They are great at showing others how they too can transform. And, as I've watched their businesses grow, these are the leaders that truly have transformed their industries.

STYLE #2: The Boss

If you are **the boss**, while you may be fun loving with friends and family, at work you are all business and you see your job as making your people toe the line. You are okay using some fear tactics to "motivate" your people. If they need it, then so be it. There is no doubt in anyone's mind who is the boss. You try to joke and lighten up the atmosphere from time to time, but you haven't been very successful so far. You know that you are not here to make friends or build relationships, you are here to get a job done and grow the business. You are frustrated that just as you get people trained, they leave and go to your competitors. You are often surprised by problems and this really frustrates you. If people would just do their job, then you would not have to deal with all the problems they create. Business success is unpredictable, and sometimes elusive. It feels like you are running on a hamster wheel, and you would like to get off.

Does this sound like you?

Let me assure you that you will find more fulfillment and less stress when you begin to take the barriers down between you as the leader and your team, and tap into their collective wisdom. It is very difficult to put your heart and soul into your business and then feel like your employees are actually working against you!

Look at the Trust Hierarchy (Chapter 3) and begin to work down each level, one step at a time. Use the Partnering Approach and create partnering workshops to work through issues together. You must work to change the dynamic that exists in your business, or you will always struggle to have even modest success.

STYLE #3: Capable Manager

If you are a **capable manager**, you are good at your job. You probably fluctuate between just letting things happen and using force when things go wrong. You don't see your job as managing the business for success, because you feel your job is making sure people are doing their jobs so that you don't have to do it yourself. You often feel overwhelmed with the amount of work you have on your plate. You sometimes feel your people take advantage of you. Communication with top management is not always open and you get very frustrated when you are the last one to know about an issue. You often resort to punishing people because you feel you have no choice. They often don't do what you tell them to do. Business success is elusive—you've had some successes, but many things aren't as successful in your business as you would like.

To improve and enjoy your business more, look at building trust with your team members. Break down the barriers that prevent your team from telling you the truth. You will have to create an atmosphere where they feel safe enough to tell you the truth. Look at the Partnering Principles and Values in Chapters 4 and 5. Incorporate some of these to create your intentions and a safe atmosphere. But don't give up and just let things happen. You can step up and lead this team to success. It takes practice. It will take time for them to learn how to trust.

STYLE #4: Good Leader

If you are a **good leader**, you value high-trust relationships, but are not always sure how to achieve them. Your people usually follow your lead but are somewhat cautious in doing so. This wastes valuable time. You encourage open, honest communication and get frustrated when people hold back. Business success is becoming more predictable when you take the leader role.

You are close to achieving the Trusted Leader abilities. You have a bit of a ways to go. Look at the Trust Hierarchy (Chapter 3) and see if you need to increase trust in your own abilities and with individual team members. This will give you the foundation to bring a new level of trust to your entire team. When your people seem cautious, ask them for their feedback. Thank them for their honesty and learn from what you hear.

STYLE #5: Trusted Leader

If you are a **Trusted Leader** you understand that it takes high-trust relationships to have an extremely successful business and team. You know that how you treat your employees is how they treat your customers and stakeholders. You inspire people to follow you and don't take advantage of their vulnerabilities. With everyone working toward a common goal, there is a strong sense of purpose and satisfaction for a job well done. Business success is becoming highly predictable in the areas where you are the leader.

While you have achieved the pinnacle of leadership, you can still work to continuously improve and increase the level of trust you have with your team, customers, vendors, alliance partners, etc. Remember, creating trust requires an ongoing effort. The opportunity exists for you, as a Trusted Leader, to help your executive leaders grow in their abilities. Sure, your example is highly valuable, but mentoring can also be very helpful to take them to the next level. Growing your own team of Trusted Leaders will produce extraordinary results for the business.

Your Intentions Matter

I am often asked, "How do I make the Trusted Leadership model, using the Partnering Approach, produce the results I want, that I see others achieving?" We often find that the leaders involved in businesses that are underperforming have a different "overall intention" than those businesses that are achieving extraordinary results using the Trusted Leadership model. It comes down to understanding your overall intention. This can make a world of difference in your results.

FIGURE 11: Your Intentions Matter

Your Intentions Matter

COMPLIANCE	CULTURE CHANGE
Focus is on TRUSTED LEADERSHIP as a Transaction	Focus is on TRUSTED LEADERSHIP as Transformational
Creates an Atmosphere of Conformity	Creates an Atmosphere of Commitment
Results in Going Through the Motions	Results in Creating a High Trust Culture

Figure 11 shows what I often see. In the left column you see the path where there is little to no real change—people are going through the motions. The intention of the leader and team is to comply with an "order or a process." Since the intention is to comply, that is what everyone focuses on. You as the leader may want to create trust and use the Partnering Approach, but your intention must be to create real change and improvement.

On the other hand (in the right column), when the intention of the leader and team is to build a high trust culture, everyone is focused on transforming how they work *together*. They are committed to changing the things that must be changed. There is commitment to having a high level of trust in everything they do. It is this intention that leads to creative problem solving, continuous improvement, and Trusted Leadership. This guides everyone along the path to creating a strong and lasting culture of trust.

As the leader you might want to ask yourself, do you trust yourself to do what it takes to achieve the high trust business that you want and need? If you don't, then start with working on that. You don't have to wholly trust yourself, because I don't think anybody on Earth does—we're all flawed. But it is essential that you improve the level of confidence you have in your ability to create trust and work with your team to achieve success.

If, in your head and your heart, you feel yourself saying, "Well, I don't know," or "I sure hope so," please remember that hope is not a strategy. Create a strategy for what you will do to learn how to use the Partnering Approach and do what it takes within your business to grow the level of trust that will be needed. You've got to do the work first. Do the work on yourself, do the work on understanding what's needed. Do the work until you feel like you have the confidence and trust that you know what to do and how to do it. The Trusted Leadership Profile can help you with that.

Your Personal TRUSTED LEADER Profile

You may have a pretty good idea of where you fall as a leader along the Leadership Continuum. Or you may be wondering where you fall. Either way, if you are curious about your Trusted Leader Style, I can help. I created the Trusted Leader Profile to help you understand and improve your leadership skills by discovering your style along the Leadership Continuum.

Your personal profile report has five sections. The first part is information about the Leadership Continuum. Part two includes your trust level and leadership style, and explanations of your style. Part three is your personal leadership descriptors. Part four is an overview of all five of the leader styles. Part five includes how you can take action for your style and what to stop or start doing.

Your personal profile report will include your primary and secondary leadership styles and pinpoint where you fall along the Leadership Continuum by giving you a Trust Level score. Your primary style is your "normal" style, and it indicates the norms you are setting in your business. Your secondary style is your "perceived" style and indicates how you believe you are leading your business. If there is a large difference, then you know you have some work to do. If you are farther toward the Feared Leader side than you would like, then you know you have some work to do. Your Trust Level score allows you to see where you fall along the Leadership Continuum from a trust level of 1 (poor trust) to 15 (great trust).

Think of the Trusted Leader Profile as a snapshot in time. You might want to take the Trusted Leadership Profile quarterly to see if you are making progress. You also might consider having everyone in your business take it and talk about their results. Or at least your leaders.

It is my pleasure to gift to you the Trusted Leadership Profile. You can access the profile at sudyco.com/profile by providing your name, business, industry, and email. You will then receive a link to the Trusted Leader Profile via email. When you have completed the profile, we will email you your Trusted Leader Profile Report.

Remember, no one is a "pure" style; we all have parts from the other styles, and our style may change in different situations. The idea is to work toward, and work to stay, a Trusted Leader, so that you create the atmosphere that leads you and your team to: (1) Get smarter—so you can tap into the collective wisdom of your team. (2) Become better—working together, aligned, and focused. And (3) Go faster—increasing your momentum so you can do more with the same resources. This can become a sustainable competitive advantage for your business. No one will be able to catch you!

CHAPTER 7:
Implementing the Partnering Approach

> *Practice daily because the quality*
> *of your practice determines the*
> *caliber of your performance.*
>
> ROBIN SHARMA

Now that you know your leadership style and where you fall along the leadership continuum, it is time to learn more about how to move along the continuum toward Trusted Leadership. The ten Partnering Principles and six Partnering Values create the Partnering Approach from which you will create your high-trust business culture. Everything you do as a leader determines what happens in your business. It's time for you to create the intentions and mindset for the culture that you want, and need, to grow your business.

In Chapter 5, I showed you how your values create attitudes and how those attitudes create behaviors. The Partnering Values create a high-trust mindset. In Chapter 4, I showed you how your intentions affect what happens. This is how the Partnering Principles shape your intentions. The Partnering Principles and Values are created in your brain by how you *think*. So, to become a Trusted Leader, you must first train your brain to think and behave like a Trusted Leader.

FIGURE 12: Four Stages of Learning

The Four Stages of Learning

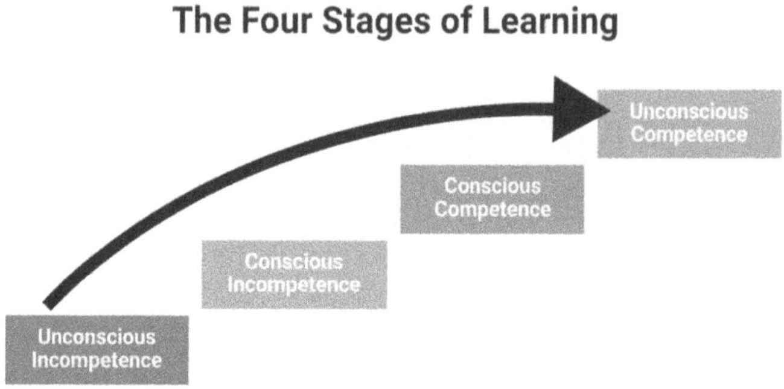

As you start on your Trusted Leader journey, please allow yourself time to grow and to learn how to think like a Trusted Leader. Martin M. Broadwell discovered that there are four stages to learning. The first stage is *unconscious incompetence*. In this stage, you don't know what you don't know, so you do what you know how to do—what you have done before. But once you learn that what you are doing isn't working, or could be better, you've entered into the second phase of learning. This is *conscious incompetence*. Now you know you don't know. You are open to trying to learn new things until you can get to the third phase of learning, *conscious competence*. This is when you know what to do and how to do it. You have become a Trusted Leader (but still have to think about what you are doing).

When you don't have to think about what to do and just automatically do all the things a Trusted Leader does, you have reached *unconscious competence*. You don't even realize you are doing these things, it has become your way, with no thought or effort required at all. Trusted Leadership is now just the way you lead and run your business.

To better understand how learning happens, think about when you learned to drive a car. At first, you had to think about every step. Turn on the car, put it in gear, adjust the mirrors, make sure no one is behind you, take your foot off the brake, etc. It was overwhelming and seemed so complicated. Today, how often do you get in the car and just drive off without having to think of anything but your destination? This is how it will be for you as you practice and learn to become a Trusted Leader. I am excited for your journey!

Train Your Brain

Your brain is a miraculous biocomputer. Just like with any computer, garbage in = garbage out. If you fill your mind with garbage, then that will be your experience of business and the world. If you fill you mind with what you want, then there is a high probability that will be your experience in the world and your business. It is your choice. Most people don't realize how they are the creators of their own experience, so they are very lax about what they allow into their mind. Unfortunately, the result is often a business filled with frustration and stress that never lives up to its possibilities.

As a Trusted Leader, you will learn to take control. You can program your mind with what you want. Here's an experiment. Close your eyes. Breathe deeply. Keep breathing. Now, visualize in your mind that there is a bucket of ice on your right-hand side. Slowly place your hand into the bucket. Leave it there. When you imagine feeling your fingers going numb from the cold, mentally take your hand out. Now, for real, feel your right hand with your left hand. Is it cold to the touch? Are you surprised? With practice, you will find that there is little difference between really putting your hand into a bucket of ice and imagining putting your hand into a bucket of ice.

That is because your subconscious mind doesn't distinguish between what is real and what is imagined. If you are thinking about how you might be late to a meeting, your subconscious mind helps you to be late. If you are thinking about how you're sure you will be on time, your subconscious mind helps you to be on time. There is a growing amount of research that shows that your brain and muscles light up the same whether you imagine something or are actually doing it.

Because your mind is programmable, you can choose to program it for what you want. You can go into any situation knowing that you will walk away with something that is amazing. I have become so sure of this that I am excited when I walk into a room filled with people in conflict. I know that we will find a way to resolve the situation; I just don't know what that solution is yet.

Unfortunately, we live in a negative world. Every day we are bombarded with news about all that is "wrong" with the world. You probably see and hear negative things about the market, a key customer, an employee, or a vendor. You may have a dashboard that highlights whatever is going wrong in your business. How can you really see the world and your business as they are, when you present such a skewed point of view to yourself? Do you listen to the news just before you go to bed at night? Do you read or listen to the latest news first thing every morning? Do you scan your email for problems you need to deal with? Think of the impact all this negative programming has on our subconscious mind, and your business.

How many times, when you have a sore arm or leg, does your mind concentrate solely on the injury? Then the pain gets worse. But if you concentrate on something else, your pain lessens. Whenever I ask people to create lists of what's working and what's not working for them in their business, 99% of the time the list of what's not working is at least three times longer than the list of what is working. Whatever we focus on becomes our reality. You must focus on what you do want, and not on what you don't want. Use your powerful biocomputer to focus on finding solutions, innovating, and growing, not on the pain of your problems.

As a business leader, you are the creator of your business, or at least the part for which you are responsible. Look into the mirror. What do you see? Is it the face of someone you respect? Is it the face of someone who takes good care of themselves? It is the face of someone who cares about others? Or do you see someone who embarrasses you? Do you see someone who has become harsh? Do you see someone who you don't care about?

If, when you look into the mirror, you don't like what you see, then you can probably also look at your business and many other parts of your life and see these same negatives. Your life and your business are a reflection of your thoughts. Your thoughts create your feelings. Your feelings create your attitudes. Your attitudes create your actions.

If your business (or life) is not how you want it to be, you can change it. If you have problems you don't want to have, then you can resolve them. It all starts with changing how you think. It starts by becoming a Trusted Leader. You and your business are not limited, except by the limitations you place on yourself. I'm sure you've heard the old tale about a little boy who heard his father yell for help when he was trapped under the car he was working on. The little boy lifted the car and his father pulled himself out from under the car. Whether this is a true story or not, in the story the little boy didn't have time to doubt himself. His conscious mind didn't have time to take over and tell him that he was just a little boy and couldn't possibly lift that car. *He just did it.*

You have absolute control. No one else has control over your thoughts but you. No one can force you to think a certain way. Only you can choose your thoughts. Only you can choose what kind of leader you want to become or what your business will achieve. But it does take practice.

YOUR DAILY PRACTICE

To train your brain to become a Trusted Leader will take practice and action. Here are six practices you can use every day to improve your level of learning, and your Trusted Leader results.

PRACTICE #1: Create a Morning Ritual

How you start your day sets the tone for the entire day, so create a morning ritual that gets you into the right frame of mind to use the Partnering Approach. Here are two steps to set your intention for the day, while also listening to your subconscious mind.

For starters, you will need a journal you can use as your Trusted Leader journal to write in. I have created a Trusted Leader Journal if you would like to use it. You can find it at sudyco.com/journal.

Write in your Trusted Leader Journal what your vision is of you as a Trusted Leader? What would make it ideal? Put in as much detail as possible. This will help your brain feel this is real.

Each morning, think about and read your ideal vision of yourself as the Trusted Leader in your business this year. Record what pops up in your mind. Go ahead and ask questions and write down the answers that come to your mind. You will discover that your subconscious will give you some great insights and ideas. Remember, your subconscious can be a source of positive thoughts, not just negative ones. Make sure you listen and don't judge.

Create a morning <u>meditation, affirmation, or prayer</u> that includes the Trusted Leader Principles and Values. You may want to record this on your phone and listen back to it. The more senses and emotions you include, the faster the learning. Or you may simply write it out and read it. Make sure you are not just talking *about* the principles and measures but *owning* them and using them to create what you want in your business and as a Trusted Leader. As you listen, or think about your meditation/affirmation, record in your journal what comes to mind. Yes, even if it is negative or seems stupid. You are starting to learn how to listen to your subconscious mind and allowing it to offer guidance. This also opens up the neural pathway for you to be able to guide your subconscious toward what you want.

PRACTICE #2: Select a Daily Trusted Leader Intention

Think about your day. What do you want to happen? What would be an elegant solution to a problem, or a breakthrough in sales, or the completion of a challenging project? What do you want? The more specific you can be the better. Write down what you "intend" to happen today. Write down how you feel now that it has happened. Who do you want to share this great news with? Write down the details of your intention. If you hear a voice in your head saying, "this is stupid," "this will never happen," "yeah sure, I can't do this," just tell that voice that you appreciate the input but you are going to listen to your subconscious for direction on what you *do want.*

Select *one* of the Partnering Principles or Values for your daily practice, the one that best supports your intention for this day. These can be found in Chapters 4 and 5. You can have more than one if you've already practiced before and achieved success. Eventually you may include several of the principles and values every day. But to start, use just one that supports the day's intention. Write it down in your Trusted Leader Journal.

PRACTICE #3: Plan for Using the Trusted Leader Intention throughout Your Day

Look at your calendar for the day. Is there a way for you to use your selected Trusted Leader Principle or Value to create or co-create your intention? What do you need to do to prepare for this? What will you say? Do you need a story to tell, or slides to share to set the stage? Do you need to make sure a specific person attends? Or do you need to talk to someone? Try to use your principle or value several times over the course of the day to create your intention. Write down where you plan to use the Trusted Leader Principle or Value during your day. Note anything you need to do to prepare and put it onto your calendar or to-do list.

PRACTICE #4: Observe and Record Response(s)

Throughout your day, as you create your intention using the selected Trusted Leader Principle or Value, observe what happens. Do you run into resistance? What was that about? What were they resisting? Do you get concurrence and excitement? What were they seeing and excited about? What did they want/need?

Record in your journal what you observe, hear, and see each time you work to implement your selected Trusted Leader Principle or Value. Yes, it can be a challenge at first to remember to record what happens and what comes up in your mind, but this is bringing what was unconscious into your consciousness, where you can take charge of what you want and leave behind what you don't want. So be patient and do the work. Remember, Trusted Leaders are "self-made," not born.

PRACTICE #5: What did you learn?

Your evening ritual can be to capture what you learned. What happened? What worked? What didn't work? What will you do differently? What did you achieve? Did you accomplish your intention? Did you create more than what you intended? How do you feel? Record these lessons learned in your Trusted Leader Journal. Go to sleep thinking of your intention and how you are on your way to becoming a Trusted Leader. You've got this!

PRACTICE #6: Repeat or Tweak?

You may do step six as part of either your morning or evening ritual, but it is important that you've had some time to let your subconscious work on your intention and understand your results before you take this step. Look at what you wrote as your lessons-learned in step five. For each one, put an X on those that you need to tweak—where you can do it better, or you learned something that will help you get a better result. Put a + next to the ones where you want to repeat what you learned. This is now a part of your Trusted Leadership arsenal. It is important to learn from your daily experiences. That is why step six is so important. If we don't learn, we are doomed to continue doing things the same way.

If you do these six steps, you will open yourself up to becoming a Trusted Leader with a reputation of being able to do the impossible! As I mentioned, I have developed a

Trusted Leader Journal to help walk you though your daily practice. The journal includes an example of a day of Trusted Leader Practice, or you can find a pdf of the example day at sudyco.com/resources.

· ·

Measuring Your Results

As you learn more, and practice being a Trusted Leader for your business, you can map your progress by taking the Trusted Leader Profile again. You can compare and contrast where you started to where you are now by looking for areas where you have grown, and at our Trust Level score. This will allow you to see the movement you are making along the Leadership Continuum. You can identify where you have improved and where you still want to improve. This can help you with your daily practice. Visit sudyco.com/profile.

I am so excited for you. If you train your brain by doing your daily practice, you will be amazed at the Trusted Leader you will become, how fast it can happen, and what you are able to accomplish. Please let me know how you do. I would just love to hear your story. You can send them to me at stories@sudyco.com.

CHAPTER 8:
What's Possible If You Use
the Partnering Approach

> *Transformation isn't a future event,*
> *but a present day activity.*
> JILLIAN MICHAELS

I have seen people transform from Feared Leaders into Trusted Leaders in a relatively short amount of time using the Partnering Approach, with daily practice. And those who didn't have as far to move along the Leadership Continuum transformed even more quickly. What I've observed is that Trusted Leaders enjoy numerous benefits, many of which were unimaginable before. Because when you become a leader that people follow, this opens doors to you that you just never thought possible.

These opportunities would not have occurred for these leaders using their old leadership style. Let me share some of the reoccurring themes I've seen happen for committed Trusted Leaders and their businesses.

Less Stress and Frustration

Trusted Leaders grow in confidence each time they are able to use the Partnering Approach to create their intention. It lessens the stress most leaders feel when things seem out of control and they spend their day putting out fires. It empowers you to *know* you can create the atmosphere for your team to co-create and implement fantastic solutions to any of the problems your business faces.

You and your team will actually begin to have fun and enjoy the business and working together. Perhaps especially when there are big problems to solve. The creative juices start to flow, and many times a problem becomes a catalyst for an extraordinary solution. Over time, when a problem comes up, you and your team will be excited to take it on, because you know that *together* you will create something awesome.

So many leaders and their teams get mired down in frustration. This is especially true when they can't get a clear answer, or the cooperation they need so that they can move forward. Instead, they sit waiting, trying to do what they can but held back by what they need. Businesses move at the speed in which decisions and answers can be provided. When your own people are not cooperating, it sets your business up to fail. Trusted Leaders create the atmosphere where people are free to identify problems as soon as possible (because of open, honest communication), so they can work together to co-create the best solution. Once the team has a track record of resolving issues, the frustration melts away because the team grows in confidence that it can resolve whatever issues come up.

Increased Employee Satisfaction

I have heard from dozens of leaders and employees over the years that they were ready to quit because their work was just too frustrating and not fun anymore. This is not the case in the high-trust culture that Trusted Leaders create. The same people have told me later that they are loving their job and it is rewarding to work together with a leader that really helps them, and the business, succeed.

I believe that this is the number one benefit of Trusted Leadership. Your employees are truly happier. If you recall, it takes choice, commitment, and cohesion to set the stage for innovation, co-creation, and success (the right side of the Leadership Continuum). That is exactly what Trusted Leaders create within their businesses and teams. When your people are happy with their job, the business, and their leader, you are definitely on the road to becoming a trusted business with a Trusted Leader. Your team will innovate and co-create ideas and solutions that no one by themselves would ever have been able to.

Customer Loyalty

Over and over, I've seen how customers will do all they can to stay with a business they trust. Even when the selection process is based simply on price, people look for ways to make it work so that they can do business with whom they want. Customers not only stay with high-trust businesses, but they also tell others about them with excited stories describing what this business has done for them.

For decades, management research has shown that how your employees are treated and how they feel gets directly transferred to customers. Trusted Leaders create the atmosphere for employees to want to care and serve their customers, because they feel they are treated that way themselves.

The cost of making sales for most businesses is a large percentage of revenue (typically 5-10% of total revenue). But what if your own team was your best sales vehicle, because of how they help your customers and generate viral word of mouth? What would it be worth to your business if your customers stayed with you for 20 or 30 years? What if you always got paid in full by your customers? That is what a Trusted Leader can bring to their business. In fact, that has been my experience for the last 35 years. We have never once not been paid in full.

Higher Margins

A high-trust business with a Trusted Leader is unique in every market sector. This kind of differentiation allows you to charge a premium. It has been my experience that your competitors will not begin to understand what you do to attract and keep great customers. But your customers will happily pay a fair premium, because they know they can trust that you will take care of them. Businesses that do not have a high-trust culture become commodities and can only compete on price.

You will earn high margins even if you charge the same as your competitors, because of the level of efficiency you will achieve by reducing the amount of wasted effort (entropy) and time. You are likely to be able reduce the level of effort required because you have great communication, coordination, and cooperation. This will drop money into your bottom line.

Part of being more efficient is increasing momentum. As your team is able to align, focus, and move together, over time they will be able to move faster and faster, and still be in alignment. This will increase the level of efficiency and drop even more money into your bottom line.

Stand Out from Your Competition

I've already shared some ways trusted businesses with a Trusted Leader(s) will stand out from their competitors. But it also seems that trusted businesses with a Trusted Leader(s) don't even need to compete. They seem to *own* their market. People come to them. Opportunities come to them.

This allows you as the Trusted Leader to pick and choose who you want to work with, how large you want your business to be, and what things you want to do. In other words, you have choices. You have control over your own business destiny.

I believe a Trusted Leader that has developed a trusted business and that also has a greater purpose for their business is unstoppable! I've seen trusted businesses that are committed to their industry or community, or to innovation, truly soar above everyone else.

Attract the Best of the Best

Like attracts like. And in turn, high-trust businesses attract the best and brightest—it is just amazing! And the best and brightest tell their friends and family, helping recruit more people like themselves. I often see several generations of people working in a high-trust business. People want to work with a Trusted Leader in a trusted business. You will have a great opportunity to select from the best of the best for your business. Make sure you are ready to select your employees from this illustrious group.

You also will be able to grow your own Trusted Leaders from within your business. They will be committed and knowledgeable, and able to create new paths to success. When you have a strong trust culture, it is best if you "home grow" your next generation of leaders. This helps to assure the continuity of the high-trust culture and leadership intentions you've worked so hard to create.

As I mentioned before, customers are attracted to high-trust leaders and their business. They will stay with you, respect you, and tell others about you. This is the legacy of a trusted business with a Trusted Leader.

Advance Your Career

Even if you work in a larger or a publicly-traded company, I have seen Trusted Leaders advance within their business very rapidly. Just this week, a Trusted Leader that has a track record of creating high-trust teams rose to become the chief engineer of a large public organization.

Businesses tend to be fairly pragmatic. If they see someone achieving consistent extraordinary results, they take notice. Trusted Leaders get opportunities to prove their abilities. Yes, sometimes that means taking on a job that seems next to impossible. But if you grow your team and use the Partnering Principles and Values to set your intentions, and continue to learn what works and doesn't work with your daily practice, you will get there—at least more than anyone thought was possible. Once you've done this enough, you and your team will have a great deal of confidence about what you can achieve. Any business (including the public sector that needs to act like a business) is going to want more of this kind of result. You will heighten your reputation and advance your career.

If you are the leader of a small, medium, or large company that is trying to create a high-trust culture, you will want to recognize the Trusted Leaders you already have and allow them to take strong leadership roles. This will support your trust culture and your Trusted Leadership role and intentions within the business. On the other hand, selecting someone whose leadership style is incongruent with Trusted Leadership will always undermine your efforts.

Become the Beloved Leader in Your Market and Industry

Trusted Leaders become beloved by their people, peers, and industry. They stand out as a beacon of trust in a sea of adversarial business leaders. I've seen it in different markets; it is the Trusted Leader that gets invited to become the industry leader. The Trusted Leader typically creates a legacy that lives on far past their time of leadership. I hear stories of how the Trusted Leader was a hero because of what they were able to do. These stories become business legends, and now the Trusted Leader is legendary! Who wouldn't want that legacy at the end of their career?

CHAPTER 9:
Wasted Energy, Wasted Opportunity, Lost Hope

> *71% of companies say their leaders are not ready to lead their organizations into the future.*
>
> BRANDON HALL GROUP RESEARCH 2015

The Seeds of Failure

There is a reason why 71% of businesses don't believe their leaders are prepared to take their business into the future, and 80% of people distrust their company. The seeds of failure get planted when leaders operate under an adversarial, protective, compete-at-all-costs, zero-sum game paradigm.

To most people, business means "bad." They believe businesses are only out for themselves and are willing to lie to get what they want. All of this is not good news for you as a business leader. What is going to make your potential customers not see you as a "typical" business leader? And what about your employees? Are you able to attract the best of the best? Are you and your team a high-performing team that creates extraordinary results? How much time, money, and energy do you waste in your business? Do you spend your time putting out fires? Feeling frustrated? Feeling like your people are actually working against you?

Remember, 70% of all new businesses fail within their first ten years. I think you have some keen insights now on why this happens. When failure is not an option, will you use the Partnering Approach to move along the leadership continuum toward becoming a Trusted Leader?

Besides fear, there is another challenge that can only be managed by creating a high-trust, partnering culture. I call it the silent business killer because I see it consistently setting business leaders up to fail.

Don't Get Undermined by the Silent Business Killer

There is a silent business killer on the loose in your business—COMPLEXITY! Complexity is what undermines so many leaders and businesses. It will undermine your growth every step of the way. It makes it harder and harder to communicate, coordinate, and collaborate. Of course you want your business to grow, but as your business grows it naturally becomes more complex. In addition, there are different subcultures within each business. You already know how Accounting operates very differently from Sales—they have different priorities, needs, and authority. You can see how complexity can become next to impossible to overcome, and why people create silos to protect their turf. If you have two people, there is one line of communication. If you have four people, you have six lines of communication. When you have 8 people, you have 28 lines of communication. When you have 20 people, you have 190 lines of communication. It all grows exponentially, so it becomes harder and harder to communicate, coordinate, and collaborate.

You must, as the Trusted Leader, have a way of melting away this complexity.

FIGURE 13: Possible Lines of Communication

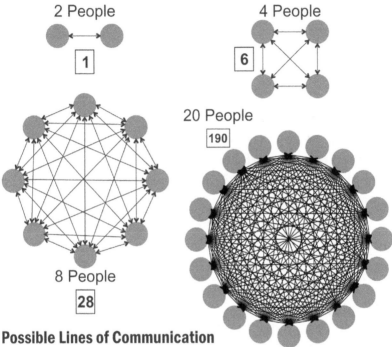

Possible Lines of Communication

The way you melt away complexity is by using the Partnering Approach (Partnering Principles and Values), to create *one* overall business team, under your Trusted Leader culture. *One* team with *one* shared, common focus that everyone buys into. Yes, this is the nozzle effect again (Chapter 2), and this is the job of the Trusted Leader. Everyone needs to know their part in the business. They need to understand and buy into the business focus, and specifically what responsibility they have in helping to achieve it. Then the actions of your team, on a weekly and daily basis, are directly related to fully executing your business focus.

If you can do this, you've got everybody marching together, and when they're marching, they might be able to even start trotting. And as they're trotting together, they might actually start to run together. And that is where you start getting huge amounts of momentum. This level of momentum comes from creating a high-trust culture using the Partnering Approach. It melts away the complexity that prevents you from being smart and working together. I think it is worth repeating: complexity undermines your ability to communicate, coordinate, and collaborate, so you cannot co-create. Tony Robbins says that "complexity is the enemy of execution."

In one example of the impact of complexity, a leader had moved his staff, files, and systems from the airport's old terminal to the new terminal at 6 pm the night before the new terminal's opening, in order to maximize revenue and minimize disruption.

Around 8 am the next day, the day of the opening, several passengers had trouble finding and retrieving their luggage. The flight information display boards were blank or displaying incorrect information. To compensate, whiteboards were put up, resulting in crowds mingling around the whiteboards. People coming to meet arriving passengers could not find their gates or determine their time of arrival. Departing passengers had similar problems.

In the meantime, passengers were not provided the boarding gate numbers that are normally printed on boarding passes. So, the whiteboards became even more important and harder to access. The same lack of information affected the airline staff, who didn't know where to report for duty.

After getting off the plane, passengers waited hours for their baggage … if it could be found at all.

Three ramp handling operators were supposed to take care of departures, arrivals, and transfer of bags. But there was no information about which carrousel the arriving bags were to be assigned to. The baggage handling system could not read some of the tags. This led to around 6,000 bags just lying around the baggage claim area.

So many people were at the airport waiting to meet arriving passengers or waiting to board their departing flights that the restrooms all overflowed. The telephone land lines crashed, so people used cell phones until that system crashed. The airport ran out of food. The doors, controlled by a fire safety system, locked and would not open. All in all, this cascading nightmare continued for two weeks until solutions were finally set up.

In short, an airport is a very complex business, and complexity creates a snowball effect that is hard for leaders to overcome, even with great effort.

These days, the sheer number of employees, contractors, and vendors needed for our businesses makes communication and decision making difficult. Add the pressure of changing requirements, tight budgets, and looming deadlines, and it is no wonder that people hunker down to protect their turf, creating silos and conflict—and all of that can erupt into chaos.

This complexity plays out in our businesses in thousands of ways. Here are a few examples.

What if the team needs a decision, without which they will be delayed and unable to move forward? How many times does the team have to stop and try to figure out who can make the decision? Then they work to try and get access to that person, only to find out that they aren't the decision maker after all, and the process starts over again. Far too often, the entire team is sitting around waiting for a basic decision so they can move forward.

What if the team gets a decision from a leader in one department/silo, and the leader in another department/silo does not like that decision because it puts an unfair burden on them? What does the team do now?

What if one part of the team is using a software program that isn't compatible with their sister team's program, so they can't share data that would allow them all to see and understand what is happening and what is needed? How do they know when there is a problem?

What if the budget changes, or the deadline changes, and the team is supposed to pivot and meet these new changes even though they were already struggling to meet the original dates and requirements? How do they reconcile these changes? What is going to give—time, money, or quality?

Complexity is part of business and business growth. Those Trusted Leaders that learn how to manage it will be the ones who are able to play the new game of leadership and become extraordinary. The Partnering Approach can help you melt away the negative impact complexity creates in your business.

Failure Looks Like Wasted Resources and Wasted Opportunities

Just a word about entropy (wasted energy, as discussed in Chapter 2). Complexity also creates entropy. But entropy isn't just created by complexity. Entropy can occur anytime you are not aligned and not going in the same direction. Whether your business is large, small, or even micro-sized, this is another challenging force that you must deal with as a leader. The effect of entropy on a business can be overwhelming. People put their time, energy, resources, and best ideas into the business. If something changes, or people were never on the same page to begin with, there is confusion and frustration.

Some or all of the resources expended have been wasted. There can be misalignments about roles, tasks, priorities, and authority. When this occurs, what one group is doing is not in alignment with another group. The business does not receive benefits from all the time, energy, and resources expended until you can get everyone aligned. Many of the resources expended just evaporate into thin air. The momentum your business needs to reach your business objectives is undermined. Below is a story of one leader's journey from entropy to synergy.

When the leader decided to use the Trusted Leader Partnering Approach, the project team was already at war with one another. The project was five-plus months behind schedule, with little to no hope that they would start building anytime soon. They couldn't get approval for their design so they could move forward. The owner was very frustrated at the lack of "quality" in the design, so they hired three levels of reviewers who continued to add comments and mark-ups to the drawings for four months.

The design team was frustrated, as they had used up all the fees two months earlier. The contractor was frustrated by waiting to get started so they could finish within the scheduled timeframe and not face liquidated damages. The week the leader started his Partnering Approach, the contractor had a load of materials that were transported to the job from 3,000 miles away arrive at 2 AM on the jobsite. The truck driver was told where to lay down the materials and proceeded to do so. Within 30 minutes, the police showed up and said they were going to arrest the driver for trespassing. Of course, the driver explained who he was and what he was doing. The police told the driver that the project manager for the owner had called and asked them to arrest him ... because the owner hadn't been told that someone was going to arrive at 2 AM with the materials.

So ... you can see that things were not going well. The leader and I met with the team, using the Partnering Approach. They realized that the entire team was new to this type of project system for construction projects (called Design/Build) and was managing the project as if it was design-bid-build (low bid price), which is a totally different type of delivery method. In design/build, the construction team is selected based on qualifications, and the designer and contractor are on the same team. For design-bid-build, the owner hires a designer and then puts the design out for "bid" and selects the lowest bidder. The contracts and payments are very different, but more importantly the locus of control for decision making is very different. There is a different set of "rules for success" in each system.

On this project, the owner expected the project to operate like a design-bid-build system when the contract and team was a design/build. So the level of document detail you would find in design-bid-build and the decision making were not aligned. This was why they ended up with three levels of review to "complete" the design documents. It was a symptom of the misalignment on the delivery system, and it was very time consuming. There was a lot of frustration within the design/build team. The adversarial nature of the relationships had gradually grown into a war … which was why the threat of arrest was made.

As the leader used the Partnering Approach, the team began to understand that they had misaligned expectations of roles, responsibilities, and how the project was to proceed. The leader took on the Trusted Leader role and committed to driving out fear and replacing it with trust. The leader held a partnering meeting monthly to get things realigned with better communication. We measured the team's progress each month using the sudyco™ Trusted Leader Scorecard. This allowed everyone to see how they were doing at following through on their commitments. The scorecard also has an algorithm that calculates a momentum score for the team. You can have positive momentum or negative momentum. The scorecard results give the leader, and the team, the means to predict what is going to occur before it happens. The team can make course corrections and steer toward success.

The owner made the decision to put in a new project manager for a fresh start. The team set deadlines for different packages to get approved. This allowed construction to move forward. When the project team learned that the owner's team didn't have all of their funding lined up yet, they successfully worked on strategies to deal with it. The leader got all the past issues resolved, and dealt with new issues as they arose. The team built momentum. The project and its team were a success. The finished bridge is beautiful, and was recognized as an award-winning project.

There was little doubt from the leader or team that if they hadn't used the Partnering Approach this project would never have been completed. In short, the project that had used up a bunch of their original money arguing over the plans, didn't have adequate funding, and had a team that couldn't even communicate well enough to deliver important materials to the site, became a successful award-winning project team (by implementing the Partnering Approach).

Trusted Leaders use the Partnering Approach. It is designed to help you create *one* team (even if you have ten divisions) that is committed to the success of your business. It is based on shared goals that allow for co-creation between all stakeholders. When you get everyone in your business focused, committed, and on the same page, complexity and entropy melt away. This trust culture will allow your team to communicate, coordinate, and collaborate, so that you can co-create solutions and decide what is best for the project and/or business. The question to ask yourself is, "How much is your business losing from fear and entropy, as well as built-in complexity?"

CHAPTER 10:
Trusted Leaders Transform Their Business

*The culture of a company is the sum
of the behaviors of all its people.*

MICHAEL KOULY

Can you imagine feeling excited and thrilled with your business? You no longer stay awake worrying at night. You are confident that you have a great team and that there is a collective wisdom you can tap into for whatever comes up. You have awesome Trusted Leaders within your business. Opportunities just seem to come to you. You have never been so satisfied with how things are going. You are doing and achieving more that you thought possible only a few months ago.

Are You Committed to Becoming a Trusted Leader?

Are you ready to let go of your old way of leading, along with the stress and frustration that come with running your business? If you never again want to feel like your people are working against you, if you are ready for much more satisfaction and success, then now is the time to act. Start training your brain to become a Trusted Leader that uses the Partnering Approach to lead and grow your business.

What may feel impossible to you today can become a normal way of doing business tomorrow, as you grow to become a Trusted Leader using the Partnering Approach to create a high-trust culture. We know that the status quo is powerful. You and your people know how things have been. And unfortunately, a sense of resistance and clinging to the status quo can limit your ability to see what might be possible. But you will learn that you and your team can do so much more than you think you can—and do it right now.

Remember that high trust = high performance. It is your job as the Trusted Leader to create a safe environment where people can share what they see and their ideas for improvement. It is up to you to create the forum for aligning everyone toward an exciting shared outcome, and to create the level of cohesion that will be needed for your team to get better, smarter, and faster. The level of momentum that you create will determine the level of success you can achieve. An inspired, cohesive team that is committed to working together to achieve success can do what others believe to be impossible.

Start Where You Are and Build from There

The next thing we must talk about is your overall business. Is your organization ready for Trusted Leadership? If your policies, practices, and processes are protective and adversarial, then you will want to start identifying those policies, practices, and processes that are in your way. But do not let this stop you from starting your journey to becoming a Trusted Leader. You can do this concurrently with using the Partnering Approach to become a Trusted Leader. You can allow barriers to "show up" as you grow your trust culture by implementing the Partnering Principles and Values within your business. Barriers are those hurdles that make it more difficult, slow you down, and disenfranchise your people—or maybe even yourself. Here are a few examples of business barriers I have encountered:

BARRIER #1: Misaligned Policy

The design team of a project spends approximately three years designing before it goes out to the construction team. The review by Construction to ensure that the design can be built is mandated by policy and usually happens a few days before the project is set to bid. This is because Design doesn't trust that Construction won't mess up their design (trust). There is no time to do a thorough review, let alone make corrections. All of this back-and-forth ends up costing millions of dollars in changes each year. It is very difficult to get cooperation between two groups when one of them feels left out of the loop.

BARRIER #2: Misaligned Practice

You need your team to identify potential problems and tell you, truthfully, about their concerns (transparency). Unfortunately, you may have an unwritten practice that no one in your business can talk to anyone more than two levels above them. Over time, the practice also includes anyone outside of your own group. A system's user, or maintainer, with a potential problem is not likely to ever get the employee's insights because the "owner" of the issue to too high up or too far away (from the employee's silo) to be able to talk with each other. In fact, in this business, you do not move up the ladder if you don't fully follow this "practice."

BARRIER #3: Misaligned Process

Let me give you another example. In a company I worked with, we finally got agreement on a set of performance measures for the company. But the data that existed within each of the company's branches did not match, because each branch developed their processes to meet their own needs and not that of the overall organization (collaboration). So, the team couldn't blend the data and understand their results. The executives got data, but if you drilled down a bit, you would see that it was different for each branch, rather than being tied together.

This kind of misalignment can happen when you have policies, practices and processes that are not in alignment with the Partnering Principles and Values. Your people (and you) will end up with a sense of cognitive dissonance. They will not be able to believe what you are saying or doing. I hear it all the time. Employees say, "Yeah, they talk about trust, but they don't actually create it." It's because you're not looking at the actual trust barriers. If you want to be proactive in identifying and tracking trust barriers within your business, a process for looking at trust barriers will be important for you.

Put together a Trust Team to identify barriers where you see poor communication, conflict, or resistance. Then work together to co-create the changes needed. This is a great way to achieve alignment, get buy-in from your key employees, and begin to have your people see the big picture, not just the picture from within their own "silo." At sudyco™ we have assisted many clients in starting a Trust Movement within their business. You create a Trust Steering Committee from people across your organization to identify the trust barriers in your business and to co-create Trust Improvement Proposals (TIPs) identifying what is needed to create trust and a specific issue. The TIPs get vetted, approved, and become policies, practices, or processes for your business.

Most organizations can do far more than they think they can. It is true that at each stage of your business lifecycle there are specific challenges you will meet. This is a natural part of growing and scaling your business. But if you can establish a high-trust culture, each stage will provide you with opportunities to grow to the next stage. Far too often, businesses succumb to the lifecycle phases and either can't move on, or die where they are. The mixture of a Partnering Intention and Partnering Values, blended into your leadership style and your business policies, practices, and processes, aligns your business. You are creating a trust culture as the underpinning of everything you do. Too many leaders and their business get trapped by their own limiting beliefs. I love the book *Good to Great*. In the book, Jim Collins shares that "good is the enemy of great." When things are going "good," you may not be so inclined to shake things up to try to make them "great," even when that means that everything could be transformed. You could do more than you imagined. Overcoming "things are good" can be a challenge for businesses.

As your business' Trusted Leader, it is important that you review your organization and get it ready for high trust. By working on that at the same time that you're building trust with your people, stakeholders, and customers, you will be building the foundation for trust to take root. Foster transparency. It will allow people to tell you things candidly, so that you will always be informed. You will likely learn things that wouldn't otherwise have been shared to you. These things might be unpleasant surprises, but not knowing simply undermines your ability to resolve the underlying issues. Trusted Leadership takes an ongoing effort. It takes commitment, especially when you just feel like blowing up or going back to your old ways. But the truth is, really miraculous things can happen. I just can't express that enough. It's a great way to work. It's a great way to lead. It's a great way to do business. It's a great way to live. And in an interdependent business world, it is the only sustainable competitive advantage.

There Are Three Levels of Trust

Trusted Leadership is a journey. It is something that you must work toward every day. It is also very important to enjoy the journey by taking note of the things that you and your business achieve. Track your progress so you can see your progression and record your accomplishments. I wanted to share with you another lesson I've learned on my journey to becoming a Trusted Leader.

How about arm wrestling with me? The objective is to get as many points as possible. Here are the rules: One point is scored for each touch to the table; no talking allowed; we have 20 seconds. On your marks, get set, go!! Wow, you are tough. I couldn't budge your arm. I'm sure glad you weren't able to get any points by forcing my arm to the table, either.

Over the hundreds of times I've done this exercise with leaders and their team, most arm wrestling pairs don't get any points, just as we didn't. But the highest-scoring pair I've ever had scored 100 points. How can this be? How can there be such a huge difference? What was our objective? To get as many points as possible. To maximize the number of points, we would have needed to cooperate and not work against each other. This is what the highest-scoring pair did. They actually changed the rules of arm wrestling to better meet the objective—to get as many points as possible. Well then, why doesn't everyone just do that? Because everyone knows how to arm wrestle. And when we arm wrestle, we are adversaries. We are supposed to try to win, or at least not lose. But because we see each other as *adversaries*, we fail to see what might be possible.

What I've witnessed as I've done this exercise is that there are actually three levels of trust:

FIGURE 14: Three Levels of Trust

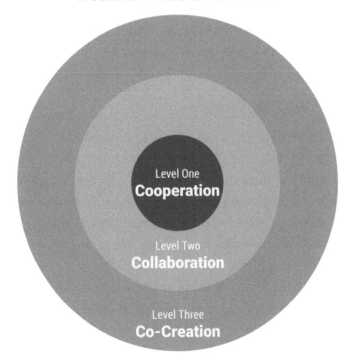

LEVEL ONE: Cooperation

The first level of trust allows us to cooperate. Here you realize that you can optimize the number of points you can get by working together. You begin to cooperate. It is one point for me and one point for you. Alternating back and forth to make sure all the points are evenly distributed.

LEVEL TWO: Collaboration

The second level of trust fosters collaboration. You have a breakthrough and realize that if we choose one side to touch (either your side or mine), we can then make even more points by being more efficient and not worrying about whose side it is. In other words, we begin to collaborate. We move our arms up and down together on the same side and are then able to triple the number of points we earn.

LEVEL THREE: Co-Creation

The third level of trust allows us to co-create. Our collaboration worked so well, we decided to really put our muscles into it and see how many points we can really rack up. So we begin to co-create points by jointly putting our muscles into it, moving our arms up and down very rapidly together (just barely off the table each time). We now earn ten times the number of points.

These three levels of trust are available to you and your business. You will move through the levels as you break down the barriers to trust. Most people stop at level one and declare victory. That is okay, of course. But there is so much more opportunity if you continue to drive the level of trust in your business to level three.

As you take your journey to becoming a Trusted Leader and use the Partnering Principles and Partnering Values to create your trust culture and embed trust into your business' policies, practices, and processes, you want to always be looking at your current level of trust. You can use your trust level number in the Trusted Leader Profile to help.

Ask yourself, are you at cooperation? Are you at collaboration? Are you at co-creation? You can keep developing deeper levels of trust. Everyone doesn't have to be at the same level. There will be areas within your business that have varying levels of trust. That is okay. Some people go faster, some go slower. That's perfectly fine, as long as everyone's on the same path and everyone knows what the overall focus is, where they're marching together toward the same goal. Make sure you learn and share lessons from the people and teams that are becoming your trust champions.

Unfortunately, a few of your people might not get there. They can't let go of their adversarial ways. As your trust culture builds, it will be obvious to them and to others that they are out of place. They often self-select out. I see this all the time. But if they don't, it is your job as the Trusted Leader to move them out, so they don't create entropy from having the wrong person in the right seat.

You Need Trusted Leaders at All Levels of Your Business

As your business' Trusted Leader, you will want to work to create Trusted Leaders at all levels of your business. You will recall that the definition of a leader is someone who has followers, and following is 100% voluntary. If you think about it, everyone in your business needs to lead at some time. They will lead a conversation, a negotiation, a meeting, a team or project, a unit or division, a channel partnership. You need leadership up, down, and in all directions to grow and scale your business. As the Trusted Leader, your people will watch and learn from you. You can also develop a mentoring program where you have more senior Trusted Leaders help those that are up and coming. You can capture lessons learned from different groups within your business, and share them so everyone rises to the new level of Trusted Leadership. With this as your intention, you can create Trusted Leaders all over your business. Imagine that!

What If You Are Not in Charge?

What if you want to become a Trusted Leader, but you aren't the one in charge, or you aren't the business owner? Are you just sunk? No. One thing I've learned is that it just takes one committed Trusted Leader *at any level* of a business to help create trust and start creating some great results. So, look around where you are. What could you do from where you sit to create trust within your team or group?

Once you demonstrate the kind of results you can create, people typically start asking how you are able to achieve this. The unique and separate culture that you create in your area can help others in the business to see what is possible. They are likely to become curious about how they can create the same kind of results for their parts of the business. Then you will have the chance to become a Trust Champion and share the lessons you've learned in your group/area.

Your Ultimate Competitive Advantage

Becoming a Trusted Leader is the ultimate competitive advantage for your business. No one will be able to match what you and your high-trust, high-performing team can do. No one will be as wise as the collective wisdom of your focused, aligned, and committed team. Nor will they be able to co-create and innovate new ways of doing old things and breaking through to new levels. You will be able to deliver faster, with better quality to more customers, while also enjoying higher margins.

I am one of those people who had to prove the value of being a Trusted Leader to myself through years of experimentation and learning. First in my own organization, then by helping over 48,000 leaders over the past 35 years, and finally by experimenting thousands of times to perfect a model so that the results become predictable. I've had the great opportunity to work with micro, small, medium, large, and mega-sized businesses that offer products and services; some are highly skilled, and some are low skilled. The Partnering Approach is proven to create Trusted Leaders that develop high-trust, high-performing businesses that can do what others believe is impossible!

In God We Trust

I have always been curious that United States currency says on the back of every bill, "In God We Trust." Take out a one-, five-, or hundred-dollar bill. It is there. Voltaire said that God created man in his own image, and then man repaid the compliment. How do you imagine God/Spirit/ Life Force/Greater Power? Artists and poets have for centuries depicted God as a human. This would make us believe that God is subject to the same frailties that we are. Maybe it is time to open the door to a new perception of God. Is your God a god of creation, trust, and good? Or is your God a god of fear and judgment?

For centuries, economics has been defined as the study of how people employ scarce resources. The underlying premise is that a society's wealth is based on its supply of physical resources (land, gas, oil, minerals, etc.), and that the world contains a limited amount of these resources. From this perspective, in order for me to gain, I must take away from someone else. If there is a finite pie, and I want a bigger piece, I must step on someone else to get it.

As I have emphasized many times in this book, way, way, way too many people believe that this is the only way to achieve business success. I know this is not the case. Business is one of our Creator's most creative endeavors. Business leaders literally think things up based on what people need, creating economic value. So many resources in our economy are not physical, but digital. We are no longer limited by geography or time. What is possible for your business today is truly unlimited. It is only limited by our own imagination and creativity. To the people who still see business opportunities as finite and scarce, I ask them to look at and trust the money in their pocket. It tells us to trust in God.

Everyone Gets Stuck

You may have people who are superbly bright, terrifically qualified to do the things you need, yet they're kind of stuck. What they could do before, they can't do now. I know for me, I suspect for others as well, the issue is getting stuck in my own limiting beliefs of what I can do, what I can achieve in the atmosphere that I'm in. It reminds me of a story that I heard years ago about some scientists who were doing some experiments with this great big aquarium tank.

There was a big pike fish inside this aquarium tank. A pike fish is just a really, really large fish. The scientists put a bunch of guppies into the aquarium. The guppies were swimming around, the pike fish was swimming around. Pretty quickly, the pike fish just ate the guppies. This happened three, four, five times as the scientists added new guppies to the tank. And then the scientists thought, "I wonder what would happen if we put the guppies inside a glass container and then put that container inside the aquarium. What would happen?" The pike fish saw the guppies, lunged for them, hit the glass, and got pushed back. Saw the guppies, lunged for them, and got pushed back. He did this maybe a dozen times and pretty soon, he stopped. The scientists left the guppies in there for a little while. The pike didn't try to lunge for them anymore, he just left them alone.

Then the scientists thought, "Well, I wonder what would happen if we took the guppies out of the glass container and put them back in just as they were the during the first experiment." So they did. The guppies swam around near the pike fish, but the pike fish never lunged again for the guppies. In fact, he ended up coming close to starving (they didn't actually let him starve). But he never lunged again.

Our minds are subject to the same kind of mental conditioning as the pike fish. We endure setback after setback, and eventually we stop trying. We stop seeing what might be possible for us, our business, our employees, and our customers. We don't believe that our dreams will ever happen. It may be time to look at how you have trained your brain to create the results you are getting. Ask yourself if you have trained your team and customers in a way where you don't get what you want. Because think about it; think about that pike fish. If he had just lunged one more time, it would have made all the difference.

CONCLUSION

Remember back to when you bought this book (or someone gave it to you)? You probably didn't know what to expect, but you wanted to enjoy leading your business more than you were. I hope you now know that this book is so much more. You can become one of the leaders that rises to the level of Trusted Leader. You can if you put in the work. If you finished the book, you learned the basics of what it takes to become a Trusted Leader and now have the tools to help you practice. If you want to learn even more, start the process over. Continue training your brain and doing your daily practice. Write down what you learn and how you have improved.

Take the Trusted Leader Profile at least twice a year. Give it to your employees, vendors, and peers. Talk about your journey of Trusted Leadership. Start a *Trust Movement* within your business so that throughout your company, people are working to become Trusted Leaders.

It is amazing that 71% of businesses don't believe their leaders are ready to move their company into the future. This is a striking statistic. Your business can rise above this and become the leader in your market segment by taking the journey to Trusted Leadership. The journey is rewarding. It is challenging. It will pull you in new directions. But it will be TOTALLY worth it! I am so excited for you.

Congratulations on becoming a Trusted Leader. Besides your business, your industry has been waiting a long time for you! You will be able to tap into the collective wisdom of your industry to solve the problems you face. Become a leader that people willingly follow. It will be leaders like you who create what is possible in business and the world in the decades to come!

GLOSSARY

ADVERSARY

A person or group you see as an opponent.

ALIGNMENT

A state of focus among people, a team, or a business, with a common purpose and commitment.

ATTITUDES

Your mindset with regard to a person or thing, including your manner, disposition, feeling, position, etc.

BEHAVIOR

A manner of behaving or acting; often a pattern based on your attitude toward something, or a given circumstance.

CAPABLE MANAGER

A leader that waivers between being fair and autocratic, and whose people do not feel seen or important. Often decisions are made by committee out of fear of being wrong.

CO-CREATION

By no longer seeing each other as opponents, but as partners, you work together to achieve synergy.

COHESION

A state of cohering, uniting, or sticking together.

COLLABORATION

To let down your guard enough to see what can be possible if you work together.

COLLECTIVE WISDOM

Sum total of the wisdom gained when a collaborative team or group is focused on a goal or problem.

CONSCIOUS COMPETENCE

The state of knowing what is required, and the ability to perform with competence; the third stage of leaning.

CONSCIOUS INCOMPETENCE

The state of not knowing what you don't know; the second stage of learning.

COOPERATION

To cooperate, willingly, with persons or organizations, who are often seen as an opponent.

CULTURE

Entails the norms that people follow within a business; based on the business' values.

EBO (EXTRAORDINARY BUSINESS OUTCOMES)

The outcome of a high-trust, high-performing team or business.

ENTROPY

Energy that gets expended, but not used for the intended goal; wasted energy and effort.

FEARED LEADER

Autocratic leader that leads with intimidation and punishment; creates a team that complies but does not engage.

GOOD LEADER

A leader seeming to be fair, who fosters open communication, but falls short sometimes. Too often, people yield to the leader and wait to be told what to do.

INNOVATION

The act of creating something new. Make changes or do something for the first time.

INTENTIONS

To design, or have in mind, something to be done or to be brought about.

INTERDEPENDENCE

The state of being mutually dependent on each other.

LEADERSHIP CONTINUUM

A scale that reveals five leadership styles between fear and trust.

MOMENTUM

The force or speed by which a team or business moves.

NOZZLE EFFECT

The result of a focused, aligned team that can achieve great momentum toward their desired outcome(s).

PARTNERING APPROACH

A two-step business paradigm that sets up the intentions and the mindset needed to create a high-trust business culture. Step one is Partnering Principles; step two is Partnering Values.

PARTNERING PRINCIPLES

Ten Partnering Principles that create *Partnering Intentions*. This entails how you act as a leader.

PARTNERING VALUES

Six Partnering Values that create a *Partnering Culture*. This involves what you believe in and creates the norms for your business.

THE BOSS

Leader who believes that fear motivates his/her people; creates resistance, uncertainty, and guessing; so communication goes underground.

TRUSTED LEADER

A business leader who knows that his/her primary role is to develop and maintain an atmosphere of trust with employees, customers, and vendors. A leader people follow because they trust them.

UNCONSCIOUS COMPETENCE

The state of mind when you no longer need to think and concentrate to understand how to do something; the fourth stage of learning.

UNCONSCIOUS INCOMPETENCE

The state of mind of not knowing what you do not know; the first stage of learning.

VALUES

A cluster of beliefs that determines a person's convictions and opinions and what they believe to be true.

TRUSTED LEADER RESOURCES

We are here to help you along
your Trusted Leadership journey.
Check out our resources at:

SUDYCO.COM/RESOURCES

Use the Partnering Approach to Become *the* Trusted Leader People Want to Follow

Imagine your business consistently producing extraordinary results that you, your team, and your customers, are excited about. Think what would be possible if you and your business were the most sought after in your market segment, and the best and brightest people wanted to work for you.

If you knew you could transform your business into a high performing team, that often does what others believe is impossible; through changing how you lead your business. Would you do it? Would you be intrigued?

The path to trusted leadership is a journey where you learn to drive out fear and develop a high trust atmosphere, so you can access the collective wisdom of your entire team, and customers. This path is put before you in eye-opening clarity by Sue Dyer's much anticipated new book. *The Trusted Leader. Use the Partnering Approach to Become the Trusted Leader People Want to Follow* reveals proven trusted leadership strategies that show you exactly how to:

- ▶ Think and Act like a Trusted Leader
- ▶ Drive out Fear with Trust
- ▶ Understand Your Personal Leadership Style and Trust Level
- ▶ Use the Partnering Principles and Mindset
- ▶ Grow a Culture of Trust
- ▶ Reap the Rewards of a High Trust High Performing Business

In addition, you will be able to create trusted leaders at all levels of your business so you can see even bigger results. Sue illustrates the trusted leader mindset with her many real-world cases where leaders have taken the partnering approach to become trusted leaders even in the most difficult of circumstances.

Connect with Sue

🌐 sudyco.com
✉ info@sudyco.com
in linkedin.com/in/suedyer

Take the sudyco™
Trusted Leader Profile

Sue Dyer developed the Trusted Leader Profile so you can better understand your leadership style and have a clear direction on where you need to go to increase trust in your business. After you've taken the free Trusted Leader Profile you will know:

▶ Where you fall along the sudyco™ Leadership Continuum

▶ How to understand your "normal leadership style" and your "perceived" leadership style"

▶ See if there is a gap between the norms you are setting and those you want in your business

▶ How to improve the level of trust you create in your business

SUDYCO.COM/PROFILE

It is recommended that you take the Trusted Leader Profile quarterly so you can see your progress!

udyco™ **CLASSES**

in Sue Dyer as you discover more about your
ersonal leadership style and how trust is the
sential ingredient in every successful business.

The Trusted Leader **CLASS**

Each free class shows you how:

- ▶ There is a continuum of leadership
- ▶ Understand your personal leadership style and its impact
- ▶ Unseen fear makes it impossible for you to lead
- ▶ Trust is the defining ingredient in your business
- ▶ Trusted Leadership is a rewarding journey

*Apply today to learn more about
mastering Trusted Leadership!*

SUDYCO.COM/CLASS

The Trusted Leader **MASTERCLASS**

A guided tour on how to become a trusted leader using the proven Partnering Approach:

- ▶ Learn why trust is the essential ingredient for all businesses in the digital age
- ▶ Spot and drive out fear before it can undermine your business
- ▶ Discover your personal leadership style and how it impacts your business
- ▶ Unpack how culture determines your results and YOU set the culture

- ▶ Use the 10 Partnering Principles to create your leadership intentions
- ▶ Create a trusted leader mindset using the 6 Partnering Values
- ▶ Learn to train your brain so you can fully implement the Partnering Approach
- ★ Get the equivalent of a master's degree in Trusted Leadership in one day!

SUDYCO.COM/MASTERCLASS

sudyco™

Bring Sue, "the Godmother of Partering" and her team, into your business to help you create a Trust Strategy and Plan to take your business to the next level!

Trusted Leader MASTERMIND

The Trusted Leader Mastermind Includes:

- Become the trusted leader for your business using the Partnering Approach
- Find the best methods to achieve your business goals
- Get tools and resources to help you build and spread a culture of trust
- Shorten your learning curve by accessing the collective wisdom of other leaders

- Watch Sue deconstruct the steps to working through barriers and problems
- Increase your Trust Score
- Do the impossible by achieving what would not be possible today
- Network and connect with other Trusted Leaders

Begin your Trusted Leader journey today!
SUDYCO.COM/MASTERMIND

Trusted Leader CONSULTING

Trusted Leader Consulting Services Include:

- Trust Gap Analysis and Recommendations for your business
- Trust Strategy Development
- *Trust Blueprint* Facilitation with your Execution Team(s)
- *Trusted Leader Scorecard* with proprietary *Trusted Leader Momentum Score*
- Trust Steering Committee Development & Facilitation

Apply today to take your business to the next level!
SUDYCO.COM/CONSULTING

BRING THE sudyco™
The Trusted Leader
PRIVATE WORKSHOP
TO YOUR BUSINESS

Bring a sudyco™ certified facilitator to your business and learn how to apply the Partnering Approach directly to your business and create your 12-month trust plan.

AM The morning focuses on each person, as a leader, and works to improve their ability to lead. You will understand what kills businesses and how to overcome these forces. You will learn the sudyco™ Trusted Leader model and where you fall along the Continuum of Leadership. You will understand your strengths and weaknesses. Then you will learn the 2- keys to the Partnering Approach. So, you can start training your brain through daily practice to think and act like a Trusted Leader.

PM The afternoon focuses on implementing Trusted Leadership within your business so you achieve specific measurable results over the next year. You will evaluate the strengths and weaknesses of your current business culture, and where you can achieve the greatest benefit from improving the level of trust. Then you, and your leadership team, will co-create a 12-month Trusted Leader Implementation Plan specific for your business.

Book your private workshop
AT SUDYCO.COM/WORKSHOP

Join Sue every week on the
LEAD WITH TRUST
🎤 PODCAST

Take Sue's wisdom with you in your pocket, car, walk or office. Each week Sue and her guests bring to you the latest tips and strategies for becoming the trusted leader for your business—no matter where you are in your trusted leader journey.

Meet interesting guests who share their secrets and struggles as they journey to become trusted leaders for their businesses and hear from experts who will mentor you to leverage what you are doing for even better results.

▶ Get fired up to start a trust movement within your business

▶ Understand how trusted leaders think and act

▶ Learn how to create a high trust business atmosphere

▶ Discover what is possible with a high trust business culture

▶ Be mentored by those who know how to build a high trust, high performing team and business

SUE DYER, MBA, MIPI has helped more than 48,000 executive leaders to create high-trust business cultures over the past 35 years. She has been called the "godmother of partnering." Sue worked on over 4,000 projects worth over $180 billion to perfect her Partnering Approach model. She is the president of sudyco™ LLC, and the author of three other books, *Partner Your Project, Working Together,* and *On-Time On-Budget.* She lives in the San Francisco Bay area with her husband Bruce, and her grandson Noah. Her daughter Jennifer is disabled and loves reading and cooking. Her son Marc, and daughter-in-law Liz, are both physicians and are very active. They have two thriving sons, Owen and Kellen.

CPSIA information can be obtained
at www.ICGtesting.com
Printed in the USA
BVHW091625020222
627778BV00002B/257